DEAR CANADA
A love letter to my country

CHER CANADA
Une lettre d'amour à mon pays

Write a season's greeting to a Canadian Peacekeeper. They would love to hear from you :
Écrivez une carte de voeux à un Soldat de la Paix Canadien. Cela leurs fera vraiment très plaisir :

Canadian UN Peacekeeper
Canadian Forces Post Office
Belleville, ON
K0K 3R0

Soldat de la Paix des Nations Unies
Bureaux de Poste des Forces Canadiennes
Belleville (Ontario)
K0K 3R0

Dear Peacekeeper / Cher Soldat de la Paix :

DEAR CANADA

A love letter to my country

CHER CANADA

Une lettre d'amour à mon pays

Les Enfants du Canada
The Children of Canada

Foreward by
The Right Honourable Roméo LeBlanc
Governor General of Canada

Préface par
le très Honorable Roméo LeBlanc
Gouverneur général du Canada

Conceived, directed and published by
Conçu, dirigé et publié par
Ben Wicks

Ben Wicks & Associates
449-A Jarvis Street
Toronto, Ontario
Canada
M4Y 2G8

Acknowledgements
Remerciements

Canadian Cataloguing in Publication Data
Main entry under title :
Dear Canada/Cher Canada : a love letter to my country
Text in English and French.
Drawings, paintings, essays and poems by 400 children.
ISBN 1-895651-10-7
1. Children's writings, Canadian. 2. Children's art--Canada. 3. Canada--Literary collections. 4. Canada in art. 5. Canada--Juvenile literature. I. Wicks, Ben, 1926- II. Title: Dear Canada.
FC60.D43 1995 971.064'8 C95-900777-6E
F1008.3.D43 1995

Données de catalogage avant publication (Canada)
Vedette principale au titre :
Dear Canada/Cher Canada : a love letter to my country
Texte en anglais et en français.
Dessins, peintures, essais et poèmes de 400 enfants
ISBN 1-895651-10-7
1. Écrits d'enfants canadiens. 2. Art enfantin--Canada. 3. Canada--Anthologies. 4. Canada dans l'art. 5. Canada--Ouvrages pour la jeunesse. I. Wicks, Ben, 1926- II. Titre : Cher Canada.
FC60.D43 1995 971.064'8 C95-900777-6F
F1008.3.D43 1995

Judging of Entries

From the many thousands of entries received from Canadian school children, volunteers selected 400 for inclusion in this book. Thanks are due to the following.

Le jugement des concurrents

Parmi les milliers de réponses reçues des enfants canadiens, les volontaires en ont choisi 400 qui sont inclues dans ce livre. Nous exprimons nos remerciements aux personnes suivantes :

 **Rotary International District 7070**

Julie Andras
Dennis Bayley
Patricia Bayley
Gordon Bennett
Richard Clarke
Brian Davis
Bernadette Donnelly
Roger Haywood
John Hemmant
Jeff Ing
Meena Jethalal
Dhara Joshi
Dinker Joshi
Beth Kates
Blema Mazin
Monty Mazin
Lorraine McKenzie
Ray Noble
Shirley Noble
Judith Parnis
Wally Reid
Lynda Ryder
Derek Tarlton
Alison Truelove
Don Voisey

A remarkable Quebecer, Joanne Dicaire, joined my staff in order to assist in the designing of this book. Without her help, the monumental task would have been impossible.

Une québécoise remarquable, Joanne Dicaire, vient de se joindre à mon équipe afin de nous aider dans la création de ce livre. Sans son apport, ce travail monumental aurait été impossible.

SchoolNet / Le Réseau Scolaire

Canada's SchoolNet provides interactive K-12 learning resources and services to Canadians through the Internet. This invaluable educational resource provides users with "single window access" to the power and reach of the Internet and its learning opportunities.
SchoolNet is an initiative led by Industry Canada and supported by provincial and territorial governments, First Nations leaders, the learning system, industry and other stakeholders. For more information, call our toll-free number (1-800-268-6608). Industry Canada and SchoolNet are pleased to have helped make this book possible.

Par l'intermédiaire de l'Internet, le Réseau scolaire canadien offre aux Canadiens des ressources et des services d'apprentissage interactifs aux apprenants de la maternelle à la douzième année. Cette précieuse ressource éducative est une «fenêtre d'accès unique» à l'Internet et à ses possibilités d'apprentissage.
Le Réseau scolaire canadien est une initiative dirigée par Industrie Canada et appuyée par les ministères provinciaux et territoriaux, les chefs des Premières Nations, le secteur académique, l'industrie ainsi que plusieurs d'autres groupes. Pour obtenir de plus amples reseignements, composez sans frais le 1-800-268-6608. Industrie Canada et le Réseau scolaire canadien sont heureux d'avoir contribué à la réalisation du présent ouvrage.

Foreword
Préface

His Excellency The Right Honourable Roméo Leblanc, Governor General of Canada
L'Honourable Roméo Leblanc, Gouverneur général du Canada

Teachers often say that they get their education from their students. And the young people writing these letters and creating these drawings have lessons for us all.

Too often, adults view the world through media which seem to shrink our horizons rather than expand them, and to disillusion rather than inspire. But when a young person sits down to write a letter or draw a picture, the small pad of paper opens a bigger world through the imagination.

Thoughtful young letter-writers in our towns and cities, in isolated farmhouses, in fishing villages, in Arctic communities, have all taken pen in hand to try to capture the hopes, dreams and essence of Canada.

With fresh eyes they remind grown-ups of our country's beauty and its tolerance and generosity. They recall to us the Canadian genius for compromise and co-operation. They teach us again why so many people consider Canada the best country in the world.

In fact, they write so movingly that their letters challenge the imagination of adults. What would we say in a letter to Canada?

Les enseignants disent souvent qu'ils ont appris tout ce qu'ils savent au contact de leurs élèves. Et les jeunes qui écrivent ces lettres et qui font ces dessins ont des enseignements pour nous tous.

Trop souvent, les adultes voient le monde par ce que leur montrent les médias, qui semblent rétrécir nos horizons au lieu de les élargir et nous désenchanter au lieu de nous inspirer. Mais lorqu'une jeune personne s'assoit pour écrire une lettre ou dessiner quelque chose, la feuille de papier ouvre un monde plus grand grâce a l'imagination.

Dans nos villes et villages, des fermes isolées, des villages de pêcheurs, des collectivités de l'Arctique, des jeunes appliqués ont pris le crayon et tenté de cerner les espoirs, les rêves et la nature même du Canada.

Avec leur regard neuf, ils viennent rappeler aux adultes la beauté de notre pays, sa tolérance et sa générosité. Ils nous rappellent le génie canadien pour le compromis et la coopération. Ils nous enseignent encore pourquoi tant de gens considèrent le Canada comme le meilleur pays où vivre dans le monde.

En fait, leurs lettres sont si émouvantes qu'elles mettent au défi l'imagination des adultes. Que dirions-nous dans une lettre adressée au Canada?

When I asked myself that question, I wanted first to get the address right. I wanted to write to a particular Canada, one that is just beginning to unfold: the country in the minds and hearts of our children.

But after "Dear Children... Dear Canada," what does one say next? Schools and parents are already teaching our children about Canadian heroes and history; about nation-building; about peace, order and good government.

Canadians have been tough enough to tame half a continent and gentle enough to provide for every citizen. But the children who wrote these letters seem to know that. They seem already to have formed an image of our past and present.

But what about the future? What guarantee do we have that Canada will remain the great country it is today? Determining that future will one day be up to our children, and they are entering a confusing world.

What message should I, or any of us, give our children about the future? I puzzled over this until I found an answer almost by accident, outside my front door.

Quand je me suis posé la question, j'ai d'abord voulu m'assurer que j'avais la bonne adresse. Je voulais écrire à un certain Canada, celui qui ne fait que commencer qu'à se dévoiler : le pays qui vit dans la tête et dans le coeur de nos enfants.

Mais que peut-on ajouter après un tel recueil? Les écoles et les parents enseignent déjà à nos enfants les héros et les héroïnes canadiens et l'histoire du Canada; comment s'est formé le pays; le principe de la paix, de l'ordre et du bon gouvernement.

Les Canadiens et les Canadiennes ont eu la force de dompter la moitié d'un continent et la compassion voulue pour subvenir aux besoins de tous les citoyens et toutes les citoyennes. Et les enfants qui ont écrit ces lettres semblent le savoir. Ils semblent s'être déjà formé une image de notre passé et de notre présent.

Mais qu'en est-il de l'avenir? Quelle garantie avons-nous que le Canada restera le grand et merveilleux pays qu'il est aujourd'hui? Il reviendra un jour à nos enfants de définir cet avenir, et le monde dans lequel ils vivent n'offre pas de solutions toutes faites.

Quel message devrais-je ou devrait-on transmettre à nos enfants au sujet de l'avenir? J'ai longuement réfléchi à cette question jusqu'à ce que je trouve la réponse presque par accident, dehors, à quelques pas de ma porte d'entrée principale.

As Governor General, I live in Rideau Hall, the country's public home. The handsome building and the grounds attract thousands of visitors. I noticed how many of them pause, and then stop to think, by the fountain just outside the front steps.

It is called the Fountain of Hope and it is dedicated to Terry Fox, the young man with an artificial leg who tried to run across Canada to raise money for cancer research and died in the effort. Terry Fox wrote a message with his life. His run was called the Marathon of Hope.

With that in mind, I would give this message to the children of Canada:

For you my greatest hope is hope itself. As you meet life's rude realities and day-to-day obstacles, may your hopes always strengthen you: the hope that we can always care for one another; that we will continue the march towards an ideal Canada; and that this country will remain what it has become, a model for the world.

En tant que Gouverneur général, je vis à Rideau Hall, la résidence nationale. Ce magnifique édifice et son domaine attirent des milliers de visiteurs et de visiteuses. Et j'ai remarqué que bon nombre d'entre eux s'arrêtent à la fontaine située à proximité des marches, puis se mettent à réfléchir.

Il s'agit de la Fontaine de l'espoir, et elle a été dédiée à Terry Fox, le jeune homme à la jambe artificielle qui a voulu traverser le Canada, à la course, afin de recueillir des fonds pour la recherche contre le cancer et qui est mort avant de réaliser son objectif. De sa vie, Terry Fox a fait un message. Son projet s'appelait le Marathon de l'espoir.

Dan cet esprit, j'aimerais transmettre ce message aux enfants du Canada.

Le plus grand espoir que j'ai pour vous est, justement, l'espoir. À mesure que vous connaîtrez les difficiles réalités et les obstacles quotidiens de l'extistence, puissiez-vous trouver la force dans l'espoir : l'espoir que nous pourrons toujours nous préoccuper du sort d'autrui; que nous continuerons de progresser en vue d'un Canada idéal; et que ce pays restera ce qu'il est devenu, un modèle pour le monde.

Roméo Leblanc

Introduction

When we decided to produce this book, our first concern was whether or not the feelings of pride in Canada had been watered down by the constant concerns voiced by many adults.

How wrong we were. More than 50,000 children across this vast land of ours grabbed pen, pencil and crayon to express the heartfelt love they share for their country.

We live in a world that is wracked with pain. Many of the children you are about to meet have experienced this pain first hand.

That the children who responded to our request know their efforts will help children in a Haitian slum demonstrates a sense of caring that will develop as they grow. We can all be proud of our country, since our children have told us that we should be.

Both Gems of Hope and The Boys and Girls Clubs of Canada will benefit financially from Dear Canada / Cher Canada. But the true benefactor of this book is the remarkable people known as Canadians.

Doreen Wicks
Executive Director
GEMS of Hope

Quand nous avons décidé de produire ce livre, notre premier souci était de savoir si les sentiments de fierté au Canada avaient été atténués par les inquiétudes incessantes exprimées par de nombreux adultes.

Et que nous avons eu tort! Plus de 50 000 enfants, à travers ce grand pays qui est le nôtre, ont pris leurs stylos, leurs plumes et leurs crayons afin d'exprimer de tout coeur l'amour qu'ils partagent pour leur pays.

Nous vivons dans un monde torturé par la souffrance et beaucoup d'enfants que vous allez rencontrer ont connu ces douleurs.

Ne serait-ce que le fait que ces enfants aient répondus à notre appel et qu'ils sachent que leurs efforts aideront les enfants d'un bidonville haitien, démontre un sentiment de préoccupation qui se développera alors qu'ils deviennent adultes. Nous pouvons tous être fiers de notre pays puisque nos enfants viennent de nous démontrer ce que signifie la fierté.

'GEMS of Hope' et les Clubs des garçons et filles du Canada recevront un apport financier de Cher Canada. Mais les véritables bénéficiaires de ce livre sont ce peuple remarquable que forment les Canadiens.

Doreen Wicks
Directrice
'GEMS of Hope'

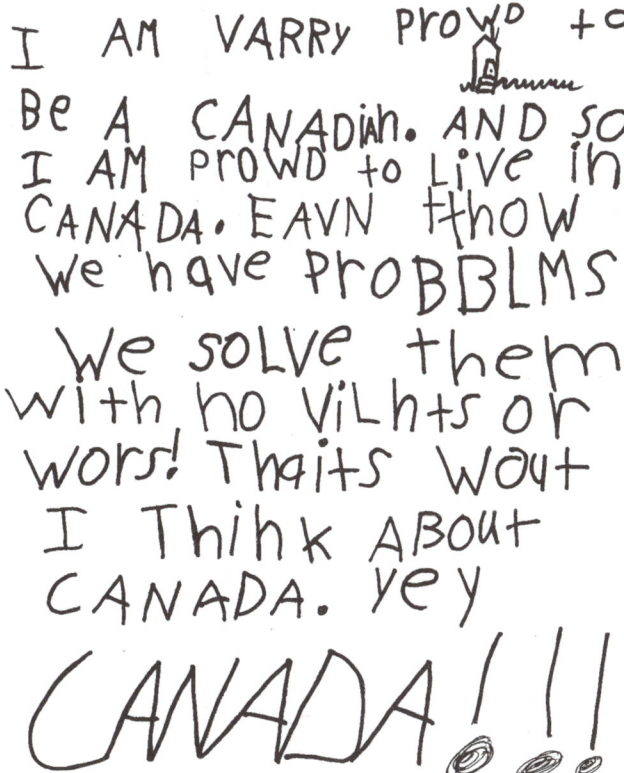

Allison Weekes, 11. St. Gabriel School, SK

Tu es un pays magnifique, le plus beau au monde. Ta nature nous montre ses couleurs brillantes; le blanc de ton hiver, ton beau ciel bleu du printemps, le vert de ton herbe en été et tes feuilles multicolores en automne.

Ton pays a de beaux hôpitaux, des magazins pleins de nourritures pour nous. Tu as de belles écoles pour tous les enfants. Celles-ci nous donne une éducation solide.

Ton pays est le pays le plus beau, le pays avec plus de paix. Ton pays est le pays qui va toujours être pour moi, le plus précieux au monde.

Annie Gaudet, AB

I AM VARRy prowp to BE A CANADiaн. AND SO I AM prowD to Live in CANADA. EAVN tthow we have ProBBLMS We solve them with no viLhts or wors! Thaits wout I Thihk ABout CANADA. yey CANADA!!!

David Proctor, 6-1/2, Burnaby, BC

9

Rebecca Routley 16, Fort Langly BC

10

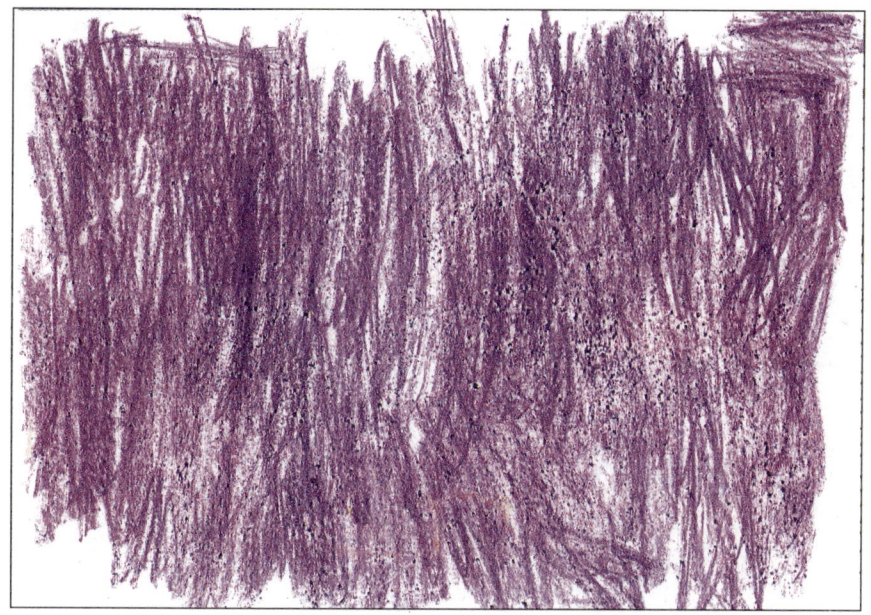

Niagara Falls by Tristen Avila, 7, ON

Fresh blue rivers flow,
Towering green trees grow.
The unearthly calls of the loon,
Colorful wildflowers bloom.

Green valleys so deep,
Snowy mountains so steep.
The vast sea shores I roam,
Canada my home.

Lindsey Horsfield, 11, PEI

Trevor, 8, Unknown

The large boat shook violently and I moved closer to Mother. We'd been on this boat for several days and everyone was tired and anxious to get off.

We left our country to escape the awful war that was raging around us. Father had died fighting that war and my little sister had died after accidently being shot when she was playing outside. Now it was only Mother and me left and we, along with thousands of other people, were leaving the country that had caused so much pain and suffering. I guess Mother was thinking about the same thing I was because when I looked up at her I saw that she was crying.

Suddenly, a small smile spread across her tear stained face and when I saw what she was looking at I smiled too. A large red and white flag was fluttering gracefully in the wind. We had arrived in Canada where we would all start a new life and try to forget all the horrors we had left behind.

Then, suddenly I felt a wonderful feeling that I've never felt before. The feeling of hope and freedom, and I knew from that day on that I'd never want to leave.

Kathryn Galvin, 14, Guelph, ON

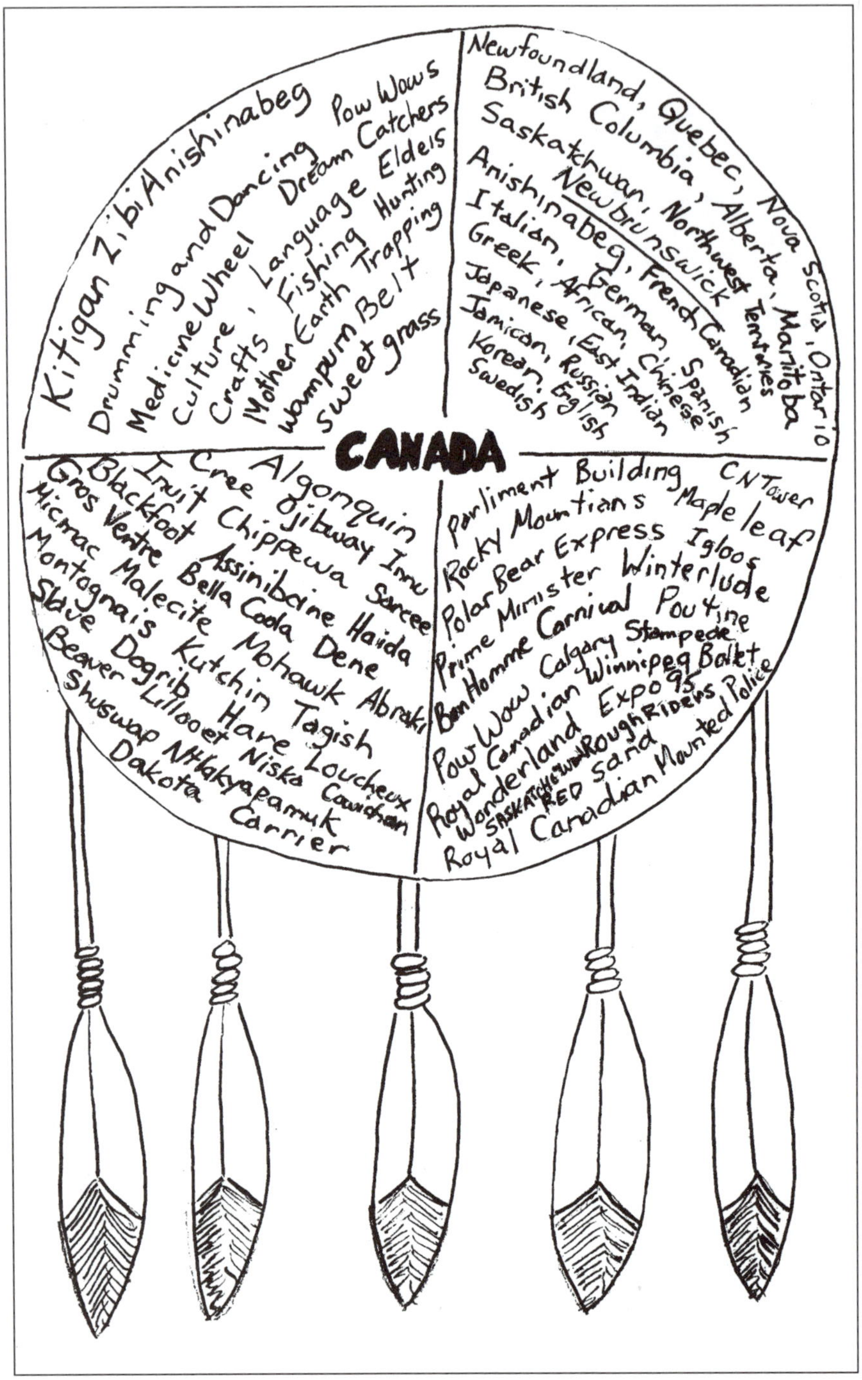

Une place où il y a l'égalité
Mon Canada
Le printemps, l'hiver,
l'automne, l'été
Mon Canada

We speak two languages here in
My Canada
A country where we live without sin
My Canada

On est protégé des guerres
J'aime le Canada
On cultive avec les bonnes terres
J'aime le Canada

Canada welcomes you with heart
I love Canada
I'm very proud to be a part
I love Canada!

Laura Jardine, 14, Oakville, ON

Although I am an immigrant
from the United States, I feel as
if this great country is my own. I
am thankful that I can go outside
and play and my mother does
not have to worry for my safety.

Christopher Cusson, 13, Placentia, NF

CANADA (dream catcher illustration)

Upper left quadrant: Kitigan Zibi Anishinabeg, Pow Wows, Drumming and Dancing, Dream Catchers, Medicine Wheel, Language Elders, Culture, Fishing, Hunting, Crafts, Trapping, Mother Earth, Wampum Belt, Sweet grass

Upper right quadrant: Newfoundland, Quebec, Nova Scotia, Ontario, British Columbia, Alberta, Manitoba, Saskatchewan, Northwest Territories, New Brunswick, Anishinabeg, French Canadian, Italian, German, Chinese, Spanish, Greek, African, Japanese, East Indian, Russian, Jamaican, English, Korean, Swedish

Lower left quadrant: Algonquin, Cree, Ojibway, Inu, Iroquois, Chippewa, Sarcee, Blackfoot, Assiniboine, Haida, Gros Ventre, Bella Coola, Dene, Micmac, Malecite, Mohawk, Abnaki, Montagnais, Kutchin, Tagish, Slave, Dogrib, Hare, Loucheux, Beaver, Lillooet, Niska, Cowichan, Shuswap, Ntlakyapamuk, Dakota, Carrier

Lower right quadrant: Parliment Building, CN Tower, Rocky Mountians, Maple leaf, Polar Bear Express, Igloos, Prime Minister, Winterlude, Bonhomme Carnival, Poutine, Pow Wow, Calgary Stampede, Royal Canadian, Winnipeg Ballet, Wonderland Expo 95, Saskatchewan Roughriders, RED Sand, Royal Canadian Mounted Police

Kitigan Zibi School, Gr. 2, Maniwaki, QC

Canada, the land of the free!
Less violence, more love.
A great country, and I might add,
It has awesome hockey teams!

Sam Pawliw, 11, Edmonton, AB

I think there are a lot of great
communities in Canada for a
child to grow up in. This is why
I am a proud Canadian.

Jennifer Irvine, 11, NS

I like Canada because it's free.

Alyse Murphy, 9, NS

Krystle Li, 9, Burnaby, BC

Stephanie McGatey, 7, Quyon, QC

All I want for Canada Day
is to catch some rays,
relax and have some fun,
and thank our Founders
for all that they have done.
Together, 128 years of unity
we will celebrate, remember
and relive, for 364 days after
this date.

Gerry Fung, 16, Nepean, ON

Lucas Deschamps, 6, Fort Frances, ON

I've heard that some people
think that Canada doesn't have
a lot to offer. There are many
places in Canada where you
can go and be at peace with
nature and yourself. I feel
about Canada just like I feel
about my friends and loved
ones. Canada is very
important and special to me. I
wouldn't live anywhere else in
the world no matter what.

Elisha Ryhorchuk, 12, SK

I am proud to be Canadian because nature is very nice.

Pascal Laframboise, 10, Yellowknife, NT

My Country

There is no place I'd rather be,
Vast land stretches from sea to sea.
Provinces are attractive places,
Many cultures make up our faces.
Free health care keeps us healthly,
Education makes us wealthly.
Our freedom of speech means a lot,
We are gratefull for all we've got.
Environmental troubles have made us wise,
Pollution emersion must be minimised.
On July 1, stand up and cheer,
And wish us many more happy years.

Jennifer Will, 13, Corunna, ON

En 1990, lorsque mes parents sont allés visiter l'Europe, ils ont voulu coucher à un hôtel dans la principauté de Monaco. Lorsque mon père a entendu le maître d'hôtel dire au client qui le précédait qu'il n'y avait pas de chambre libre, mes parents ont pris leurs valises et se sont apprêtés à partir quand le gérant a remarqué un drapeau du Canada collé sur l'une d'elles. Il leur a demandé de le suivre et leur a affirmé qu'il lui restait encore une chambre. Il a déclaré qu'il ne ferait cela pour personne, autre que des canadiens, car il était allé a la guerre et des Canadiens l'ont aidé à combattre l'ennemi pour qu'il ait ensuite la paix.

Isabelle Aucoin, 13, Moncton, NB

In school, I look up at the flag hanging over the door.
Why do I love Canada? Just because I live here? No, much more.
Look around you, open your eyes.
What you see shouldn't come as a surprise.
You see a rainbow of people all under one sky.
You're included in this rainbow, you and I.
A haven to save people from hunger and strife.
A place where those people begin a new life.
What about the people who were here before?
We are now united. From each other we learn more.
A place to be free, to soar like a bird, to rise.
A land where we try to see through other's eyes.
One sun, one moon, one earth on which we stand.
We share with the world our love, our peace. Hand in hand.
A country where no one at all is ignored.
A country where no possibility is left unexplored.
Be whatever you want to, say whatever you will.
There's no one to die for and nothing to kill.
And the sun will be left to drown in sorrow.
No one will be left to drown in sorrow.
Escape to the ocean and take a free ride.
Stand on a mountain. Feel good inside.
More diversity than any other place in the world.
A place where every story can be unfurled.
I look back at the flag hanging high above,
And I realize that it simply means love.

Stephanie Szakacs, 12, Edmonton, AB

Gérard Patrick LeBreten, 8, Dundee, NB

I am deeply honoured to be a citizen of Canada. You see, when I was little I always wanted to be someone I'm not, but now since I realized how lucky I am to be Canadian...! Just different cultures get together and make a better tomorrow for us all makes me happy.

So I am writing this letter not to whine but to show people how lucky they are and I will try and do my best to make Canada a nice place by picking up litter or something.

Kristina Fredeen, 10, Chilliwack, BC

Lisa Laflamme, 12, Montreal, QC

Lisa A. Lubenskyi, 12, Boucherville, QC

Isabelle Larochelle, 16, St-Basile, NB

We have a very special family, with an English and a French parent. We come from both these cultures. Without each other, we're not Canadians or Canadiens. It's like we've been tied together by laws and politics as well as highways and railroads. If we can't cooperate, our country falls apart. It makes me very, very sad because we can't compromise. We'll fall apart because we've forgotten that we're actually better together.

My dear Canada, this is why I'm your dedicated little patriot. I am a lover of beauty and majesty, of history and origins, or multiculturism and diversity. I'm a lover of peace and freedom and both our parents, no matter how different they are. Maybe I've forgotten this for a while, but it's that I remembered that counts, and that I can inspire others to do the same. And I'm not ashamed to scream my dedication from the rooftops because, my beloved Canada, I can't contain what I feel for my nation and I want to give some of it back. Call it enthusiasm. Call it devotion. Call it the energy of a Canadian youth.

Angela Eykelbosh, 14, Stony Plain, AB

Cher Canada,
Je t'aime beaucoup.
Tu es mon ami
Et merci pour tout.

Mélanie Boyd, 9, Dartmouth, NS

17

My sentiments billow beyond my prudence; I simply can't conceal them any longer. It would be remiss of me not to share them with you. Surely you wouldn't mind, you have always heard me out before.

My heart was captivated by you the moment I was born.

Certainly "Love At First Sight" is more than a fairy tale. You didn't hold me tightly in a grip of bondage. Such an ungodly way simply is not in your nature... it never will be. Instead, you cradled me gently in your strong steady arms, and sang lullabies to me of peace, freedom and contentment.

I was taught by my parents to never judge a book by its cover, but your beauty made me believe otherwise. Your sparkling waters, stately forests and majestic peaks overwhelm me. Others have come close, but none have surpassed you. Your acceptance, sweet and enduring, drove me closer to you. You have looked upon many, black and white, and made room that others will learn from your example.

As a host, you are charming and gracious. Your house is lovely and neat. Your table laden with bounty. There are always enough chairs around it, for you, my love, refuse no one. You are giving and forgiving, wise and winsome. Your fragrance of freedom allures so many.

You have drawn me to you and called me your own.
Oh Canada... I love you!

Heather Anne Haxton, 15, Cochrane, AB

Angie Dinkel, 14, Lanigan, SK

I love you because you are one of the richest countrys In the world and you have lots of food. We have forests for wild animals. I would miss alot of stuff if I lived Africa.

Jon Kornelsen, 7, Cut Knife, SK

Je suis contente de vivre ici, cher Canada. Je suis ravie que tu ne m'as jamais montré la guerre et que tu m'as toujours montré la paix.
Cent remerciements pour être née dans un de tes hôpitaux et pour avoir pris soin de moi. C'est grâce à toi que nous avons des vêtements et de la nourriture à mettre sur la table.

Céline Dickner, Falher, AB

Sara Jenkins, 11, Rothesay, NB

J'aime la liberté
Que tu m'a donnée
La vie est très belle
Ici au Canada.
J'aime les sports variés
Que tu nous présentes à
chaque saison
Tu es le pays le plus beau
Je ne vais jamais te quitter
Et continue ton bon travail
Je te remercie.
Cher Canada.

Wendy Merchant, Falher, AB

If you were visiting Canada,
you'd know it was Canada
because we're just... nice.

Katie MacArthur, 9, New Minas, NS

In my picture each marble represents a culture. I have made them all brightly colored to show how each one is different, but no better than any other one. I chose marbles to represent cultures in Canada because they can exist close together without all changing to become the same.

When you look at the different colored marbles together they look alot more appealing than if only one color was in the bag. I feel that it is the same with people. I love Canada because it is a multicultural country.

Andrea Wheeler, Gr. 8, Edmonton, AB

I like to listen to the breeze
While I am sitting in the trees.
In PEI I saw some whales
And then we saw some beaver tails.
We walked along tidal flats
We also saw some mountie hats
I love to watch the Canada Goose
As much as I do the big old moose
I love to sit beside the sea
With nothing, no one except me
I love to lie and watch snow flakes
Fall onto the ice cold lakes
Canada is a great place to be
I love it and it loves me.

Laura Hendrie, 10, Guelph, ON

Canada I Love You!

Darrell Graham, 13, Canterbury, NB

I don't know how much I love you Canada, but thank you, thank you, thank you. Even if we are having some trouble with the Canadian dollar, it's better than having thousands of little cities and towns that no one wants to live in because they're in the middle of nowhere. We only have maybe 4 or 5 of those and people still want to live in them. Well, I think I have written enough...

Kevin Villiers, Gr. 5, Calgary, AB

Troy Holloway, St. John's, NF

I hope this collage (which I decided to do because my drawing sucks) gets in on time.

Margaret Li, 14, Calgary, AB

I am a chinook coming up from Calgary;
I am a new born baby named Gary;
I am a farmer combining wheat;
I am a butcher cutting meat;
I am a tornado in 1987;
I am a saskatoon pie hot out of the oven;
I am a football game in the park;
I am a welder who is making a spark;
I am a waterfall honeymooners love to see;
I am a refugee from war seeking safety;
I am a rancher riding a horse;
I am a pilot in the CANADIAN air force;
I am a poppy "Lest we forget";
I am a fisherman casting a net;
I am a pack of wolves hunting caribou;
I AM A CANADIAN HOW ABOUT YOU?

Daniel Hawkins, 11, Edmonton, AB

You Are my world I LOve you

Susan Fok, 5, Laura Secord School, BC

Canada you're a red crunchy apple that tastes good.

Robert Blackhall, Gr. 5, Surrey, BC

I am French and I am English. I have lots of friends.
I hope Canada does not separate.

Andrew Desjardins, Gr. 2, QC

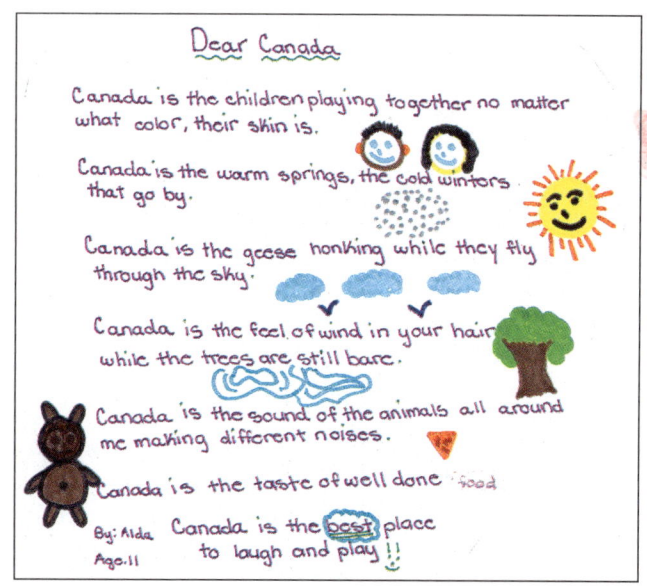

Dear Canada

Canada is the children playing together no matter what color their skin is.

Canada is the warm springs, the cold winters that go by.

Canada is the geese honking while they fly through the sky.

Canada is the feel of wind in your hair while the trees are still bare.

Canada is the sound of the animals all around me making different noises.

Canada is the taste of well done food

Canada is the best place to laugh and play!!

By: Alda Age 11

Alda Tavares, 11, Manitoba, AB

Rebecca Oliver, 17, SK

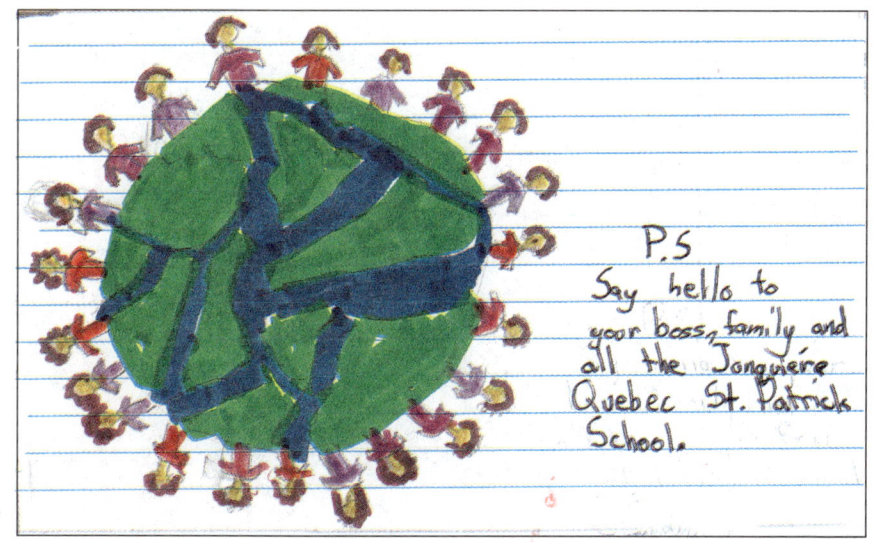

Jeffrey Cassie, 7, École Cité de l'Amitié, NB

P.S
Say hello to
your boss, family and
all the Jonquière
Quebec St. Patrick
School.

Cindy Tremblay, Gr. 4, Jonquière, QC

Dear Canada,
I hope everything
is ok. And nobody
gets hurt.

Mariella De Ciccio, 7, Laval, QC

Canada should be kept beautiful
and peaceful and together... the
number one country in the world.
Le Canada est un pays spécial...
S'il vous plaît restons ensembles.

Felicia Biondi, St-Léonard, QC

I love your beautiful scenery of flowers blossoming and river water running. I love to watch the beautiful sun rise and sunset in the cool weather of spring and I love going to the warm beaches in the summer. Going ice-skating is fun in Canada with a breeze brushing across my face. I mostly love you because you're very colorful, but what I think is best about you is that you're a free country where everyone can be friends.

Allison Weekes, 11, St. Gabriel School, SK

Patricia Yu, 9, Charlottetown, PEI

Le Canada est tellement beau,
Le Canada notre coeur si gros.
Our country has no fear,
For hope and happiness are all here.
Le Canada une place pour tout,
Le Canada pour moi et vous.
The friendliness in the air,
Are like the lakes so crystal clear.
Le Canada une place sans guerre,
Le Canada avec ses grosse mers.
We're world renowned for our hockey greats,
A country since birth, that's been on its skates.
Le Canada les montagnes si hautes,
Le Canada la nature sans fautes.
Even when dark, our spirits bring light,
We unite together, no reason to fight.

Ava Kolodziej, 14 & Andrea Wallace, 13

All my friends are here

Derick Wong 6, Vancouver, BC

I JUST want to give Canada a big HUG!

Heather Lippold, 9, Calgary, AB

24

Leif Menezes, Gr. 5, Calgary, AB

Captain's log...

We are looking for a country to live on. The Commander Finnigan says, "Haw 'bout Australia!"
It is beautiful with koala bears. Finnigan says, "Koalas are not bears!"
Then Doctor Sarry says, "How about China? They have a lot of bikes and great food."
Captain Morris says, "I heard about Canada. If we get there in time, we could get there for Canada Day."

Anthony Morris, 12, Roslyn School, QC

Mom and Baby Polar Bear

Darcy Lane, 6, Calgary, AB

I love CANADA because it is special.

If there was no CANADA I think I wouldn't be as happy - I feel free and a bit sad - because not everybody knows how good it is to roam free and to grow up in such a beautiful country.

CANADA I love you and I always will!

Ariana May Giroux, 9, St-Hubert, QC

I like canada becuase we get summer and winter. I like canada becuase i like the big big mall thank you for my mom and dad. thank you for my brothers thank you for my cat.

Rulie Marzyk, 8, Dauphin, MB

Catherine Pino, Redvers High, SK

Nadia Bujold, 13, Balmoral, NB

One day I took a garbige Bag to school and cleaned up the school gronds. I did it to help the invierminte. I had to wear gloves. I wish that other peple wod clean up too. I don't like garbige.

Dan Lane, 7, Calgary, AB

26

A maple leaf sky
A tree overhead
A robin sets fly
Where a squirrel just fled
An ant on a leaf
A bee on a flower
Above a small reef
Of puddles from a shower
A robin is bathing
Itself in a pond
With fluttering and waving
Ah, now it is gone
A chipmunk is racing
Itself round a tree
And soon it is facing
and noticing me
As I sit in a chair
With a pen and a card
And write poems about
My... Canadian backyard.

Elyse Jean Graham, Delta, BC

Darcy Lane, 6, Calgary, AB

The grass is green, leaves are brown, sky is blue, people all colors. We have a lot of colors in the world. One color... I don't know.
Please God, what color is love?

Zahra Goodarz, 9, Calgary, AB

Erin McQueen, Saskatoon, SK

Amy-Lynn Goodfellow, 14, Newcastle, NB

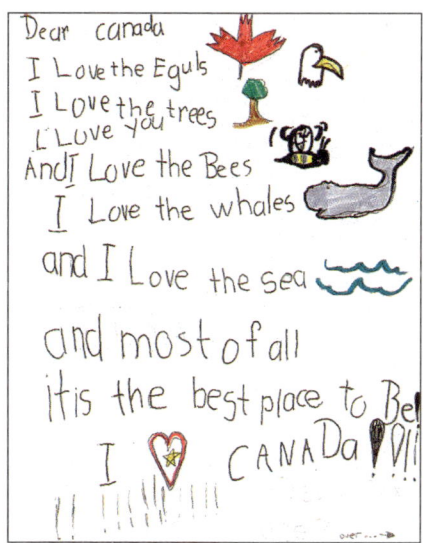

Dear canada
I Love the Eguls
I Love the trees
I Love you
And I Love the Bees
I Love the whales
and I Love the sea
and most of all
it is the best place to Be
I ♥ CANADa!!!!

"... without a speck of help!
First poem ever!"

Devin Cox, 7, Delta, BC

Canada's Essence

A land where hope and
happiness,
Echoes through the hills,
But though full serenity,
Canada is not still.
A home to many races,
A place for friends and kin,
With raging, roaring rivers,
And quiet valleys to wander in.
Quiet and tranquil,
Beautiful and free,
A place of hope and gladness,
For all eternity.
If someone split this country,
And put our land at risk,
Somewhere inside these borders,
Good people would resist.

If famine creeps across the land,
And crops rot in the ground,
Always there will be someone,
To make a joyous sound.
Our mountains will protect us,
Our forests will stand tall,
The cliffs will tower above us,
And make a mighty wall.
The seas and lakes and rivers,
The ponds and brooks and streams,
The hills and fields and mountains,
Are like unto a dream.
Canada so wonderful,
Canada so free,
Canada a land of hope,
United unbreakably.

Evie Farmer, 12, Acme, AB

Anita Baidwan, 11, Richmond, BC

Dear Canada,

How are you feeling? I know you must not be feeling too good with people dumping trash on you all the time. In our school we have a recycling program to help decrease the pollution in your beautiful lakes, rivers, forests and mountains! I pick up all the trash that I see in the woods and I see floating around in the water. I hope I did a good enough job for you!

Your friend,
Fred Mooney

P.S. Could you try to arrange for good weather in our area this Saturday, because I'm going fishing!

Fred Mooney, Placentia, NS

Brittney Beckett, 4 or 5, Kings Co., NB

I love the parks that you have. They are so big that every day I go and play in them. I always go on the swings and my father pushes me. When I am on the swings I go so high that I reach the sky.

That's all I have to say Canada so bye.

Adlene C. Cappuccino, Gr. 2, QC

I have lived in Canada all my life and plan to keep it that way in the future unless the unemployment rates increase.

Dana Whittle, 13, NF

Dear Canada,

I haven't stopped thinking about you since I moved to America. My heart has broken with the pain of solitude. I long to hear the crashing of the waves at Peggy's Cove in Nova Scotia, to feel the caress of the soft southern wind, to see your many beautiful sunsets. I am not writing this letter for your sympathy, but to tell you how empty my life is without you. If love were tears I would cry you the Hudson Bay, if love were wind, I'd give you a dozen tornadoes. There's no other country that can make me feel the way you can. I love you.

Anne Hopkins, 12, St. Stephen, NB

Tommy Spike, 12, Paviliou, BC

I like Canada. I am French and English. I have lots of friends both English and French too. I hope Quebec is always a part of Canada and that they don't separate.

Steve Ryan, Gr. 5

If there was no such thing as canada, I don't think I would be as happy as I am now! I am happy because most men put their work into building side walks and are fixing up water pipes also. They are making roads easier to drive on.

Desneiges Campbell, 10, Calgary, AB

Valérie Perreault-Murphy, 12, Longueil, QC

And with this beauty,
We should all understand,
To carefully protect,
This unique land.
Although we don't know the future,
We've seen the past;
We know what Canada is,
And we want it to last!

There's so much more but it just won't fit,
This poem describes just a little bit.

Stephanie Finlanson, 12, Caledon, ON

Emmanuel-Fortier, 14, Pokenouche, NB

32

Canada

We live in Kitigan Zibi Community. We fish for our food. We make dream catchers and medicine wheels.
Casey Cote

We love Canada so much. We like to hunt animals. In Canada, we are the Anishinabaes. With moose skin we make moccasins. We go to Pow Wows. We make birch bark canoes.
Kerri-Ann Marchand

We love Canada. We hunt for animals. We love Pow Wows. We love the water in Canada. It is so nice in Canada. We make jewelry. The trees smell nice.
Gloria Decontie

We hunt for rabbits, bears, moose and deer. We eat the meat. With their fur, we make moccasins and other crafts.
Cameron Cote

We love Canada. At Pow Wows, my mom sells bracelets, necklaces and earings that she makes. I help my mom to make them and we sell everything.
Amanda McConni

Kitigan Zibi School, Gr. 2, Maniwake, QC

Diana Xu, Vancouver, BC

Dear Canada. Cher Canada

Canada yo're the nicest place I had been to. I'm born in Yugoslavia and I came here becuase of the war and now I almost like it here more than in Yugoslavia. I feguered out that English is realy easy to lurn. I do miss my fiends in Yugoslavia but if I went back there I would miss my friends here. Canada is a special place.

Milos Coko, 9, Calgary, AB

Tammy Lee Walsh, 12, Wellington, PEI

FREE AT LAST

As I looked out the window,
It occured to me,
That Canada was the place to be
With birds gliding up in the sky,
Making pretty little cries.
The trees stretching out, all about
Makes me feel like making a
happy shout.
This is a great place, unlike the war,
There is still some crimes which we
Don't adore.
I'm an old lady which I have dreams,
Some have come true, without a clue.
When I was small, my family was poor.
Many were killed in the war.
But we have moved away from the past
And we are finally free at last.

Daphne Cheung, 11, Sarah Wong, 10, Takako Murakami, 11, Seneca Hill P.S.

Top 10 Reasons to Live in Canada

10. Our screwy government
9. The pride shared among the people who live in Canada.
8. Our money isn't green.
7. Rated number 1 country in the world.
6. The history.
5. The food.
4. It's cold.
3. It's home.
2. The Tragically Hip live here.
1. It isn't America.

Darren Scheuer, 12, Ripauin, SK

So I guess now that everything else has been put into perspective, it's time to say what I started writing this letter for. All other "three little words" aside, I love you, Canada. How could I write so many good things about a country I don't love? And I'm sure I'll feel the same way in the middle of February when my house is covered in snow. I'll even feel the same way when the GST is raised 30%. Even if Mulroney were to become PM again, I'd still love you. Because I know what country it is that I call home, and I know where to find the best Mexican soft-taco with extra chili powder outside of Mexico. Where else but the world's own, Canada.

Julie McIsaac, 15, Hamilton, ON

Mary Catherine Alice Blagrave, 11, NB

Something that makes me upset is when people complain because they can't get a new bed, or they can't get the treats they want for lunch and they have to have potatoes and vegetables. I wish they would realize what they do have.

To me Canada means a warm place to sleep at night, good food to eat and lots of freedom. My dream is to never have any wars. I hope that it can happen soon.

Cassie Spencer, 11, Elliot Lake, ON

You make me happy because you have monkey bars.

Dicky Wu, 5, Vancouver, BC

The Maple Leaf Forever

We strive for national unity
Where man abides in harmony
Where freedom rings from sea to sea
Canada, land of liberty.

The maple leaf that's known worldwide
An emblem of our nation's pride
Every day we love you better
Hail the maple leaf forever.

Andrea MacNeill, 8, St. Stephen, NB

May the red maple leaf live forever and may Canada always be a great place to live.

Michael Collins, St. Edward's Elem., NF

When I think of Canada,
I think of people free,
Of forests filled with animals,
And vast amounts of trees.
When I think of Canada,
I think of mountains high,
Of lakes where beavers live,
Beneath the clear blue sky.
When I think of Canada,
I see hockey on the ice,
And baseball players on the field,
Who've been world champs twice.
When I think of Canada,
I see our mounties ride,
A flash of red to music,
They hold our flag with pride.
When I think of Canada,
I think of people proud,
To be of different cultures,
Many faces in the crowd.
When I think of Canada,
I think of Niagara Falls,
The natural wonders of our land,
Not just shopping malls.
When I think of Canada,
I see the great Sky Dome,
I see a place that many people,
Can proudly call their home.

K.C. Mountjoy, 12, ON

Lukas Archer, Gr. 5, Calgary, AB

Jonathan D. Grant, 17, Canterbury, NB

My country's important, I know that at the least
It's great for taking long walks on the beach
It has provinces, count them or believe me there's ten
Nova Scotia, New Brunswick, Newfoundland, PEI
Visit these places and on their beaches lie
BC, Manitoba, Alberta, Saskatchewan, too
Grass that is green and a sky that is blue
Northwest Territories, Yukon don't forget
Which provinces have we not mentioned yet?
Quebec and Ontario are great places to go
They're both places in the middle of Canada, you know
So there you are, with Alberta's oil
Our nation, Canada, also has Prince Edward's soil!

Kelly Hunter, 11, Mill River, PEI

Kimberly Byrd, 12, Montreal, QC

Kwey!

We love Canada because it is a beautiful country. In Maniwaki, Quebec, where we live, there are wonderful lakes and lots of fish. There are moose and deer that we hunt in the fall.

We appreciate that the Canadian government pays for our school. It's a great school. At it we learn about our Algonquin language and our heritage. We learn to respect our elders, and how to drum and dance. Also, we learn how to survive in the bush and make dream catchers. Our school has really modern computers, a big gym and cafeteria, and lots of lockers. In Canada we have lots of freedom. Canada is a good place to live.

Màdjashin (Grade 5, Kitigan Zibi Kikinamadinan)

Aaron Beaudoin, Nick Commonda, Dustin Coté, Jeremy Dumont, David Sutherland, QC

Yasmeen, 10, Calgary, AB

Mon pays est comme un rubis qui brille au soleil. Il n'y a pas de guerre et les gens nous acceptent tel que l'on est.

Véronique Côté, 10, Ste-Françoise, QC

Jennifer Little, Harvey High School, NB

J'aime beaucoup le Canada parce qu'il y a de la lumière qui nous éclaire. J'aime beaucoup le sable chaud qui ressemble à des milliers d'étoiles tombées du ciel en petits morceaux. Il y a aussi de l'eau qui nous est très utile pour se lasser nager et boire. Nous sommes chanceux de vivre dans ce beau pays. Alors arrêtons de polluer cette terre qui nous est très chère et respectons là.

Kristine Cassidy, 9, Shédiac, NB

WHY CANADA IS THE BEST ↓

1. Its number 1
2. We have the freedom
3. We are not racism.
4. Not a lot of killer diseases
5. We respect other people (ELDERS)
6. Hardly any pollution
7. THERE IS PLENTY MORE Reasons why we LOVE CANADA BUT There is no more room on the paper.

Love
Elizabeth Jeffery & Linda Arsenault.

Elizabeth and Linda, Iqaluit, NWT

39

Marilyn Tardif, 11, Chatham, NB

40

I love my country because it is peaceful and quiet. We are keeping bees and they just love it here because they have lots of nature to explore. It is fun seeing nature like apple trees growing. In my backyard we have an apple tree. I play on it a lot. I can get to the top of it, it is very fun.

Please help me keep it this way.

Alexandra Pook, 8, Riverport, NS

Corinne A. Mallonga, 8, Vancouver, BC

Juliane Gallant, 9, Shédiac, NB

I'm Proud to be A canadian That's it, That's Final That's All. We don't need Las Vagas to have A ball.

Paul Zammit, 11, Sydney, NS

My mom and dad can now provide my sisters and I with much more than what my grandfather provided for his family. He came to Canada with only the clothes on his back. Canada gave my grandfather a home and gave him a chance to work to give us a bright beautiful future. I can see the look in his eyes when he watches me that he is happy and joyful of his accomplishment. Thank you Canada for making my grandfather proud.

Daniel Mendola, Gr. 5, Burlington, ON

I think that living in Canada is like watching the sun go down with your best friend.

Sara Turner, Calgary, AB

Dear Canada
I am writing you a love letter because I get to go to school. We get to bike ride and we get lots of food. Good bye friend.

Renée Thunderchild, 6, Prince Albert

I wanted to do something for you, something more than just write poems and letters. Then I realized that there is something I can do. I can use all you have given me, your support and your beauty, the gifts of your abundant resources, and I can use them to my advantage. I can become a good person, and I can help others. That is what you do, and that is what I will do, because of you.

Tyler Speer, 15, Edmonton, AB

Coreen Villamayor, 10, Vancouver, BC

En 1991, j'ai traversé mon pays en voiture, ce magnifique pays appelé Canada. Je l'ai traversé d'un océan à l'autre en appréciant chacun de ses aspects. Avec ses dix provinces et ses deux territoires, le Canada forme le plus grand et le plus beau pays au monde (d'après moi).

Christine Aucoin, 11, Moncton, NB

The whisper of the south wind,
Slips through your better being,
Bringing stories of smiles and successes,
This is Canada
The sun's luminous ray,
Stretches over a world of opportunity,
Where dream's night sky is dotted with the stars of reality
This is Canada.
Where the solo song of love,
Is sung hand in hand,
Humming the chorus of peace and memories of old,
This is Canada.
Where nature's symphony
Is spread over vast plains and dense forest,
And the music rings loud,
For they are one and we must listen,
This is Canada.
Where the mountains stand in regal beauty,
Giving us the power,
To live and love like the ones before us,
Where peace is unconditional, for we are all equal,
This is Canada.
Where people eat and sometimes do not think,
That others are dying because of something so plentiful,
But those who do think care and maybe that is best,
This is Canada, the land I love.

Brianna Johnson, 11, Calgary, AB

I love you Canada because you are giving us the most important thing, "your love." When I grow up I will give you the best of mine.

Marlyn Felaya, 10, East York, ON

Alicia Reeves, 6, Wellington, PEI

Canada, Canada,
   is the place,
 Different people of different   race.
Lots of food grows from
the ground, we can
share it all around.
We can sing and we
can dance, we live in
Canada, we have a
chance.

Tayla Fraser, 8, Bassano, AB

Brian Russell, 11, Bonavista, NF

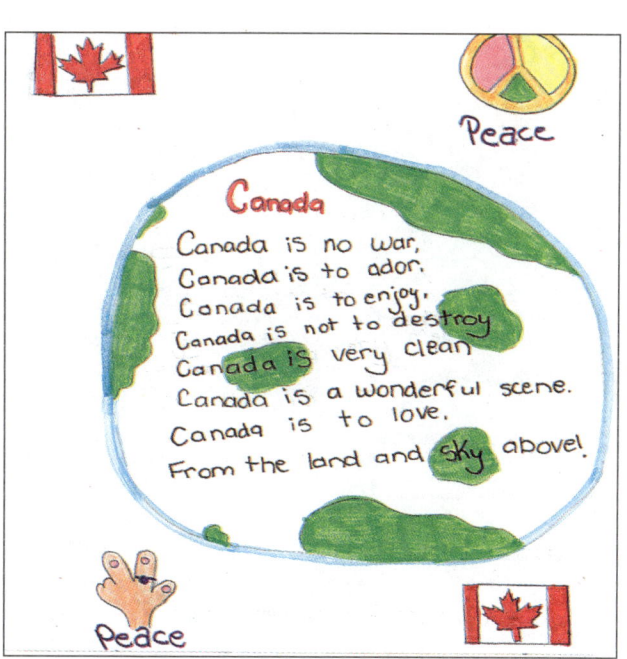

Angela Possberg, 11, Humboldt, SK

Who I am is a game we play
Hope your guess won't take all day
I'm red, brown, green and gold
All of the above I am told
You can find me on a nickel or penny
You know me if you have any
I'm born in the spring and die in the fall
Get your rakes one and all
I'm blue or white at the Gardens or away
It's our national game we like to play
My many points you can see
Represent the provinces from sea to sea
So hoist your flag and let it unfold
The maple leaf mystery now has been told.

Kathryn Kane, 11, Lunenburg, NS

Mary Claire Boudreau, 10, New Waterford, NS

Brandy Pakkala, Gr. 8, Cambridge, ON

Impressions of Canada

As you cross this vast endless country,
Of one hundred years ago, and more,
You see the Yukon's passage,
Of gold rush days that are o'er.
As you pass through this fast growing country,
In a time when the railroad's at work,
You'll find Chinese men blowing tunnels,
A job that all others would shirk,
As you traverse this strong spirited country,
Through the west, woolly and wild,
You see many people ride horses,
From elders to a little child.
As you stand on this country's vast prairies,
The flatness, stretching for miles,
All you can see is dry yellow,
And sometimes, scattered hay piles.
As you trek through the country's great northern,
O'er islands and tundra so vast,
You wonder, with blizzard winds blowing,
How the Inuit manage to last.
As you look at this many laked country,
You see the greatest stand fast,
Superior, Huron and Erie,
Beautiful, ever to last.
As you see this bilingual country,
Where the French have a land all their own,
Though the Abraham battle was first fought,
Quebec is a province called home.
As you view this historical country,
The oldest white men which we know,
The Vikings who came from Norway,
Helping this country to grow.
As you find this incredible country,
The islands along the east coast,
With lighthouses, fishboats and always,
The farmland, a beautiful boast.
To discover this wonderful country,
You must look at it all, not just part,
And as closely you look at the people,
You see peace of mind, steadfast heart.

Heather Buckley, 11, Calgary, AB

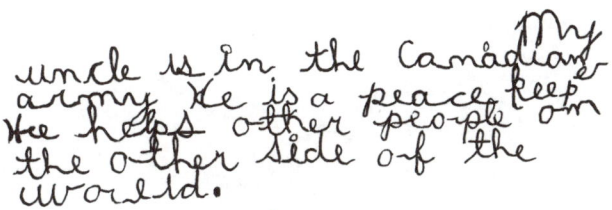

My uncle is in the Canadian army He is a peace keeper He helps other people on the other side of the world.

Jeffrey Mills, 7, Stoney Creek, AB

Dear Canada

mountains towering

wheat fields rolling like the sea

clear waters flowing

Janet Hill, 11, Calgary, AB

"God's Country"

Chris Ennis, 11, Placentia, NF

47

Alex Li, 12, Burnaby, BC

I emigrated to Canada when I was five. I was born in Indonesia and then moved to Hong Kong when I was one and a half.

When I was in grade three and my brother "Michael" was in grade six, everything was perfect until my family found out something was wrong about my brother. He had cancer, a brain tumor. When my mother told me the bad news, all I could think of was that he was going to die. Soon afterwards, Michael couldn't talk and needed a wheelchair and tons of medicine. After about nine months his condition got so bad that he needed to be admitted to the hospital and two weeks later he passed away.

But during those times the love and help of doctors and nurses and the people around couldn't have been better. My school even arranged a counselling program for me while my brother was sick.

My mother still can't get over the fact that my brother died so she goes to the bereaved meeting where she shares her experience with other families who had lost a member of their family too. It really helps my mom, and she says it helps her to heal. So I guess what I love most about Canada is the helpfulness and love in everyone, the beautiful scenery, the weather and the laws. And I hope it will never change.

Michelle Li, 10, Vancouver BC

Save Canada because it's the only Canada we have and if you don't, it will be polluted and smelly and I won't have time to play!!

Jennifer Kemple, 11, Calgary, AB

I love you because you and Me Have the Same birthday

Martha Overbeek, 6, ON

HERE IS A PICTURE I DREW OF MYSELF PICKING FLOWERS FOR MY DADDY OFF THE TOP OF A HILL. I LOVE CANADA BECAUSE IT IS SO PEACEFUL LIVING HERE.

Tianna Macleod, 6, Rchd. Co., NS

To me you're like a wonderful painting of many bright colors beautifully sitting side by side. The colors are your people that bring their cultures from other countries and all these cultures come together in wonderful unison.

Krissy Brady, Gravenhurst, ON

From the days of John Cabot in the 15th century to Jean Chretien in the 20th century, Canada combines the history and pride of the old world, with diversity and progress of the new world. Canada stands for courage of brave people of the past, the heritage of Natives, French and English, of peace makers and keepers of the future. Like murals, many new cultures combine to keep Canada strong and free, with dedication to serve humanity.

Leon Menezes, Gr. 5, St. John's Fine Arts School

I am a Proud

Canada is a beautiful country,
A land of vast resources,
New home for many people,
A symbol of democarcy,
Defender of others in need,
In wars, fought for freedom,
A trusted ally for the U.S.,
Never give up spirit.

Stephanie Currie, 11, Calgary, AB

I love Canada. There is no wars in Canada. Most people have food and homes. In Canada we are secure and there is not many stealers. I love Canada most because it's blue and green and Canada is my home.

Shannon Greer, 7, Calgary, AB

Robbie Bailey, 11, Vancouver, BC

50

Abra Hamilton, 13, Smithers, BC

I like my reserve because there is a lot of swimming areas. I like my reserve because people know each other and they speak to you and you speak to them.

Kyle McGregor, 9, QC

Your waters sparkle like the eyes of your proud preserves and defenders. Your lands are so green. It's breathtaking. Your country is full of freedom and multiculturism. The flag of your country shines within our hearts, the colour so bold and beautiful. The provinces within you stand tall and proud to be part of your beauty. Your mountain ranges run coast to coast for all of your admirers to delight in. You're known for welcoming strangers with wide open arms. That is why I love you so.

Elyse Boudreau, Gr. 5, Robin Foote School

Some of us are trying to make peace but others are trying to make war. We should give peace to one another.

Kimberly Barry, Gr. 3, Placentia, NF

51

Emily Gray, 9, Fort Smith, NWT

Country of mine, the freedom you possess.
Liberation to believe what you believe and to choose the panoply in which you dress.
You are a bountiful goddess bestowing gifts among your subjects.
Justice, truth, beauty and love have molded you into a dynasty no one rejects.
Ancient rivers course through your pristine terrain,
Gracing the beauteous land with fertility purling as they came.
The turbid seas on your either side
Enclose your interior where diversities of land reside.
The lush forests flourish with spicy hopes
while the lazy prairie rolls and rolls and more or less lopes.
The mountains like amulets of living silver shimmer bright
While tides ebb and flow from the shore glow with froth and moonlight.
In places where poverty and oppression reign
The people dream of heaven where there is truth, liberty for all and peaceful lanes
In reality, Canada is what they yearn for many a year.
Oh Canada, dearest Canada, where we know no fear.

Larissa Wodtke, 12, Winnipeg, MB

Trina McMullen, 12, NS

Tu es grand, tu es beau on est chanceux de vivre dans cette jolie place. Les personnes ici sont gentilles.

Christina Blair, 13, Oakville, ON

Cher Canada:
J'aime mon école parce que
J'ai beaucoup d'amis
J'aime mon lapin

J'aime canada

Steven Koncan, 7, Huntsville, ON

Lucas Kurztkowski, Edmonton, AB

CANADA

How can one country
Be mother to many?
How can a nation be human?

How can one country
Be a teacher to all?
How can it be like a person?

How can one country
Be such a worker?
How can a country be living?

Canada raises us,
Canada instructs us,
And Canada builds us,
That's how a nation can live,

Because she is beautiful,
Because she is caring,
Because she is free and strong.

So we are her children,
All of us are,
And she treats us as equals,
No matter how different we are,

Our Lady, Canada.

-Jessica Laura Miller

Jessica Laura Miller, 13, Williamsford, ON

Canada Forever

When it's cold and wet outside,
I don't care, I take pride,
In what I see surrounding me.
Canada is the place to be.
In wintertime the trees are bare,
Mom makes you wear long underwear.
In the fall we play ball,
And in the spring we sing.
In summer it's hot, hot, hot.
I feel like a cooking pot.
I go out to the swimmingpool.
I think it's really rather cool.
This is my very last rhyme.
In Canada, every day is fun time.

Kelly Durnford, Gr. 3, Calgary, AB

I like Canada because you don't have to use tooth picks and cotton instead of Q-tips...

Kavita Sharma, 8, Abbotsford, BC

I think Canada is nice because there are no kings.

Justin, 9, Cochrane, AB

Thank you Canada for being the country you are. All of my friends came from different places. Natsuko came from Japan, Thomas came from Croatia, Natasha M. came from South Africa, Crista came from Italy and all of my friends are great!

Kathleen Susak, Home Schooling, BC

Jason Marroni, 9, Valleyfield, QC

54

We Are Canadians
Nous Sommes Canadiens

We just got started,
Not that long ago,
We are still a young country,
But we have much to show.
Our world reputation,
Is one of the best,
Our nation is peaceful,
And one full of zest.
We have many inventions,
We help stop the wars,
And with world contributions,
There's much more in store.
Our country is one,
Of all religions and race,
We are all one nation,
Where no one's out of place.
Nous parlons l'anglais,
Et le français aussi,
Nous sommes heureux,
Et nous aimons la vie.
Notre héritage merveilleuse,
Est pleine de fièrté,
Quelquefois nous avons perdu,
Mais souvent nous avons gagné.
La campagne est très belle,
Nous avons des montagnes et
des champs,
L'eau est clair et propre,
Et la nature est importante.
The Mounties are our guardians,
Our elders are our guides,
Our achievements have no limits,
So reach for the skies.
We are all Canadians,
So stand tall and proud,
Let the world know,
Shout it out loud,
Nous sommes Canadiens!

Jeannine Guindon, 13, Arnprior ON

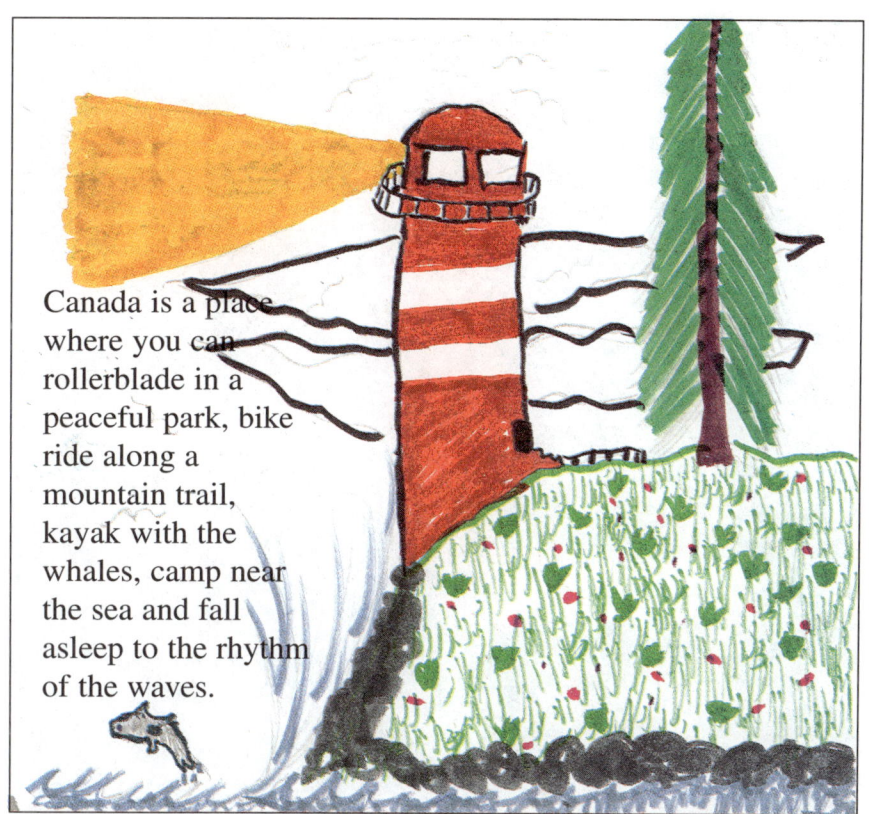

Canada is a place where you can rollerblade in a peaceful park, bike ride along a mountain trail, kayak with the whales, camp near the sea and fall asleep to the rhythm of the waves.

Jessica Torode, 9, W. Vancouver, BC

O Canada so free and fine
Of all the things it gave to me
It gave me fresh air
So don't you dare
Take my country away from me

Blaine MacInnes, 11, Glace Bay, NS

Anna Tkachenko, N. Vancouver, BC

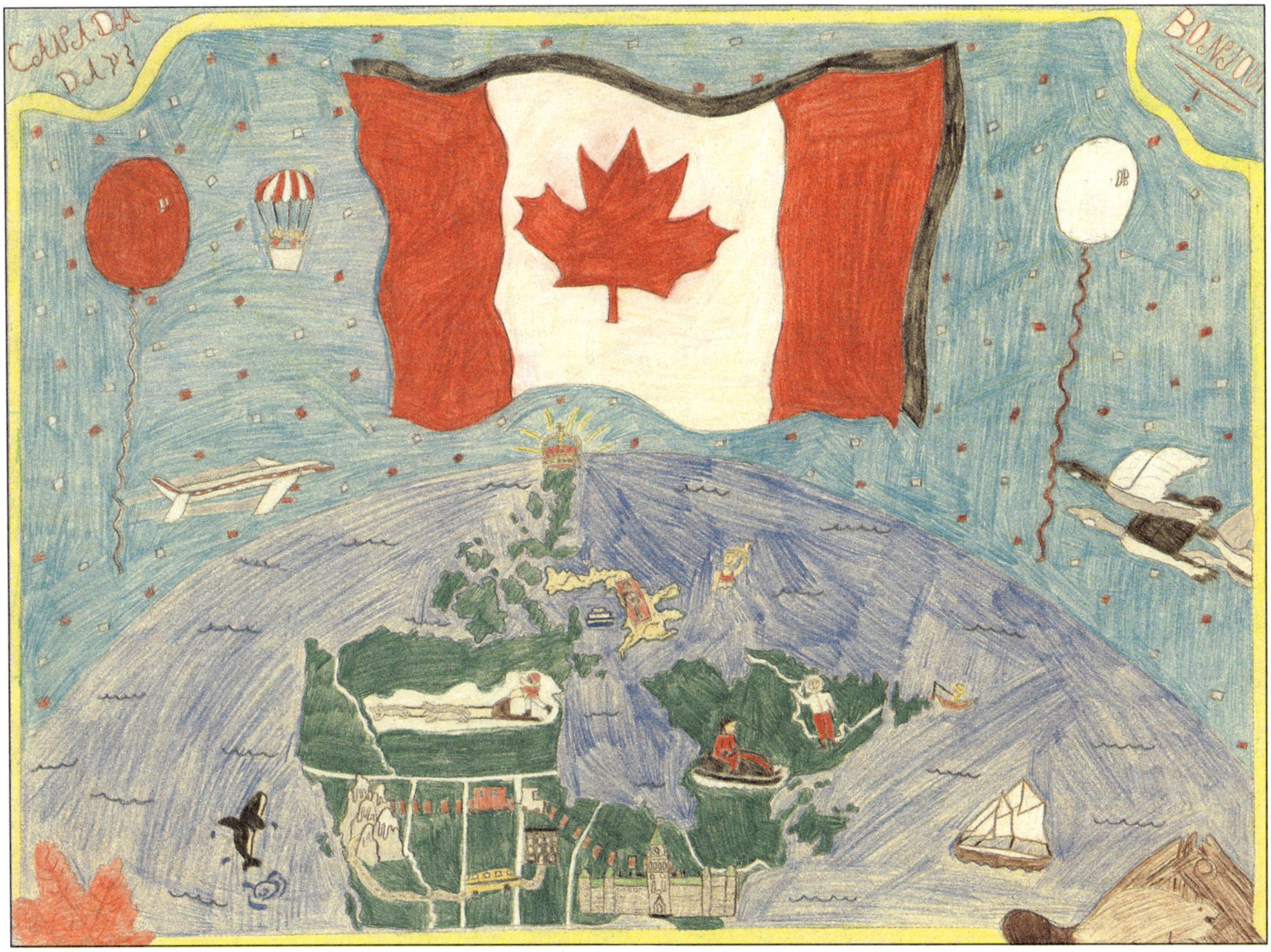
CANADA DAY!
BONJOUR

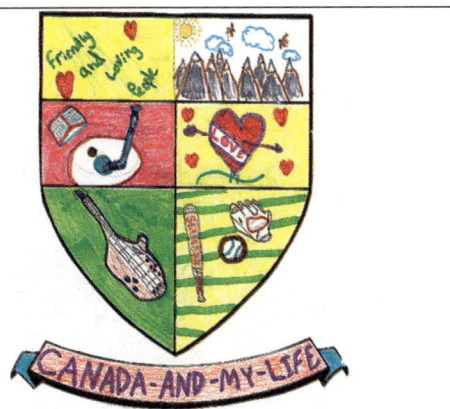

Janel Boone, 11, Bonavista, NF

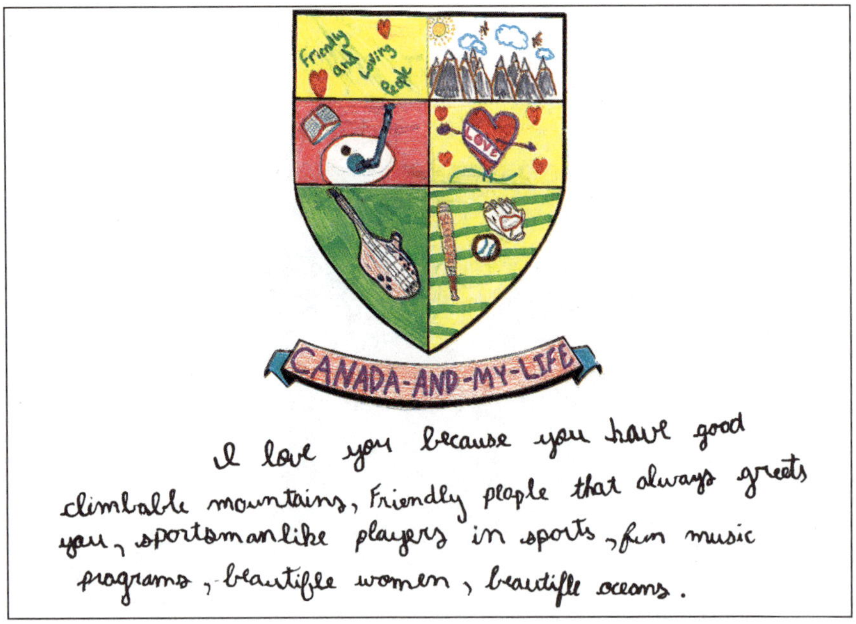
Friendly and Loving People
LOVE
CANADA-AND-MY-LIFE
I love you because you have good climbable mountains, Friendly people that always greets you, sportsmanlike players in sports, fun music programs, beautifle women, beautifle oceans.

Wayne Forward, 11, Lunenburg, NS

You are not only my home, but also my bodyguard against the whole world. You are my wealth, my love, my life.

Sure you have your downside but you are where I will always be at home. I was born here and I shall die here. So Canada can be built on top of my deceased self for-ever more.

Marena Winstanley, 11, Vancouver, BC

I am happy to live here. I was Kidnapped in the U.S. when I was only 18 months. My mother thought that canada was nicer and safer. We have lived here for nearly ten years. I have not been Kidnapped here. Thank you. I think that you are the best. I hope you stay that way for ever.

Alicia Martinez, 11, Ottawa, ON

Alfred Étienne, 13, Montreal, QC

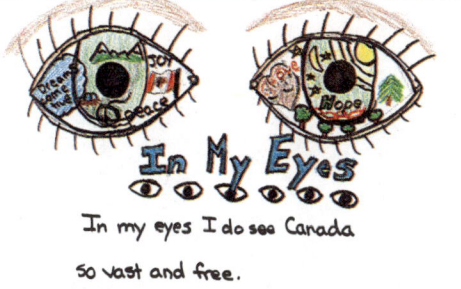

In my eyes I do see Canada
so vast and free.
In my eyes I do see a land
that cares for me.
In my eyes I do see people
living in harmony.
In my eyes I do see a flag that
flys so gracefully.

Kay Linley, 11, Rosemont School

Le Canada c'est un pays merveilleux!
Voir le drapeau dansant dans le vent heureux!
Les cultures différentes sont comme sur une plage-sable
Ici dans notre pays du feuille d'érable.
Cette grande terre d'immigrants qu'on aime et protège
Dès les régions de pluie jusqu'au Grand Nord de neige
Est couverte en paix, et nous sommes fière.
"Merci pour ce pays!" dison-nous, en prière.
J'aime surtout tous les célébrations
Qui démontrent la fidelité du nation.
Les autres nous pensent un pays amicale.
Et c'est ce que nous somme, mais pas grâce aux terres.
Le Canada c'est le jardin, mais nous sommes les fleurs!

Emma Kate Vetsch, 13, Edmonton, AB

I am happy to live on you because you are free and we can vote for our leaders.

Stephen Greene, 8, Placentia, NF

My friend Emilsa came to Canada last November. She moved from Guatomola because of the war. She can't speak English very well but out of the words she could say, she described Guatomola like this : hide, scary, bang, boom, kick, tank, help. I understood her clearly of what she was trying to say. Our country is free.

Laura McMahon, 10, Niagara Falls, ON

David Namkung, 11, New Westminster, BC

Dear Canada,
You know there is racism. I try not to be but it makes me sad that other races make me mad. I do not know why or how, but I know you shouldn't be of any thing like that because I think they are rich driving their cars when some Indians don't have one. I know this is the start of racism. I don't like to think that I may be racist, but I know I am not.

Sara Favel, 8, Burnaby, BC

DEAR CANADA

Dear Canada how lucky we are to be

Living here in the land of the free

No fear of war as we move around

Fresh water and air here are always found

Free to speak and worship any place

Regardless of your color or race

If only all the children of the world could be

As lucky as the ones living in this country

Danielle Mossman, 7, Lunenburg, NS

I am sending you this letter because I love you. My name is Mathew Kuandibens and I am an Oujibua Indian. We are one of the Indian tribes that first lived here.

The thing I like about you is all the scenery and all the parks and wildlife. I also like that there is not much violence on the streets. I don't like all the pollution, all the cars and all the trees being cut down. But I still like all that's nice, and the fact that it's free to live here.

I don't like all the racism that's going on. Well, I still love you anyway.

Mathew Kuandibens, Gr. 4, Surrey, BC

Canada, Canada you are the best in north, south, east and west.

Canada, Canada I love you from my ribbon to my shoe.

Canada, Canada you are so great, if you had a girlfriend you vill have lots of dates.

Jessica Pang, 8, North Delta, BC

Dear Canada
I love you because
it snows in the winter

Melanie Thompson, 10, Edmonton, AB

Canada is a place of FREEDOM
Canada is a place of PEACE
Canada is a land of HARMANY
and a land of good PENPIE

Josh Manitaoyen, 11, N. Battleford, SK

60

Svea Rawe, Edmonton, AB

May we please come and immigrate in your beautiful country?

Yes, of course. We as Canadians are proud to know that people from other countries want to immigrate in Canada

Asia

South America

Europe

Africa

Australia

Amanda Rasmussen, 12, Jonathan Lemmond, 11, Matt Young, 11

Canada is a place of many cultures
Joined together as one great nation
And together, side by side, friend to friend
When we share our backgrounds
And respect those of others
A peaceful happiness if formed
We must preserve this happiness
So that we may hold our heads high and say -
"Bienvenue au Canada, un pays de liberté"
"Welcome to Canada, a country of freedom"
And speak it proudly as the truth.

Amrita Roy, 12, Burlington, ON

Here's a joke... Once upon a time there was a place called Boyitoba. What was his name when he grew up? ¡Manitoba!

Scott Neufeld, Gr. 2/3, Clearbrook, BC

61

Canada, the one and only....

Soaring birds, deep blue sky, all these things are in my eye.
Tall, tall mountains up above; this is just half my Canadian love.
Bold eagles can really fly! I hope Canada will never die.
Canada is one big place; to me it is no disgrace.
If dreams can really come true, I hope Canada is still in you.

Megan Martin, GR. 4, Surrey, BC

Canada, you are the best
Because of you my heart's at rest.

Andrea Miller, 8, ON

I wish the Canadian dollar would be worth more than the American dollar because if it was, we could give the people in Haïti even more money.

Lloyd Kovacs, Calgary, AB

Jessica Winsor, 12, Labrador City, NF

Dear Canada,
I love you because you are very nice and you take care of me. You are a nice country. My mom and dad love you too. My sister loves you too. I hope all the bad poeple will stop being bad. I will clean you up. I will tell my friends to clean with me. I love you a lot.

Clean up Canada we need it.

From Adrian.

Adrian, Johnsview Village P.S., ON

Mon Pays

Mon pays Canada
Est un pays marveilleux
Des océans profonds
Jusqu'a les montagnes très hautes.

On y trouve des castors.
Et de gros cariboux
Des forêts et des abres
Qui pussent partout.

Il y a quatre saisons
Ils sont tous differents
C'automne. l'été. l'hiver
et le printemps.

En Yukon il fait trés froid
Mais en Ontario
c'est tres chaud
pour moi!!!

En été on fait du camping
On joue. on nage. on va
à la piscine.

Emyle Connell, 9, Hamilton, ON

Laura Lam, 12, Brossard, QC

Ali Leier, West Vancouver, BC

I CAN SOAR

Your embrace...

    I feel like a fledgling, so safe and secure,
    In a nest lined with feathers as soft as fur.
    I feel so confident and wonderfully strong,
    That I want to break out in sweet joyful song.

Your freedom...

    On wings of freedom I swiftly soar,
    In pursuit of dreams I'm striving for.
    I'm as free as the sky, the wind and the sea,
    And nothing, oh, nothing could ever stop me.

Your beauty...

    What a wonderful country to look down upon,
    From the West Coast so green to the prairies of fawn.
    From the bleak white far north, to the sparkling Eastern sea,
    Your beauty never ceases to overwhelm me.

    Your beauty gives me strength as a very young bird,
    While freedom entices me as I mature.
    Your beauty will inspire me forever more,
    Canada, Oh Canada, you make my heart soar.

Audra Mitchell, 10, W. Vancouver, BC

Jill Viejou, 10, Gravenhurst, ON

Here in Canada, I think criminals and murderers who rob banks and stuff like that should lighten up.

Tara-Lynne, 10, Grand Bay, NB

Oh Canada, is a country dear,
Where all our people have no real fear.
Women and children have a chance to grow,
To be equal, schooled, and in the know.

Lynda Bailey, 14, Richmond, BC

Chris Polanski, 12 & Roman Maslej, 12, Etobicoke, ON

Sure you think wherever you live is the greatest place but I wasn't born in Canada. I was born in Croatia and I say Canada is still better. That's why I believe Canada is a great place to live.

Mark Lovrekovic, Kitchener ON

Canada is the best because we don't brag like other countries (well, except me).

Colin Boyne, 10, Saint John, NB

We don't want Quebec to go away
So please Quebec with us stay
English and French are languages we speak
Without that we would be weak

Tara Nichols, 13, Sarnia, ON

Canada is a cool place...

Sara Powell, 8, Oliver, BC

Cher Canada: J'aime les animaux que tu m'as donné. Merci pour toute la liberté.

Mariève Héroux, Hunstville, ON

So you're a Canadian, eh?
What does that mean?

It doesn't mean you live in an igloo or wear a lumberjack coat or play hockey or listen to CBC radio or watch "Road to Avonlea".

So you're a Canadian, eh?
What does that mean?

It means a rich heritage, hearing both "welcome" and bonjour", respecting diversity of culture and religion. It means opportunity, an abundance of food and clean water, quality education, universal health care, tolerance, freedom and pride.

So you're a Canadian, eh?
What does that mean?

It means you're lucky.

Lisa Lemieux, 15, Edmonton, AB

THE RAINBOW COLOURS OF CANADA

RED
- the colour of the maple leaf which represents the whole of Canada as one independent nation. The colour of the bloodshed and vigour that united Canada as one whole ; both socially and politically. The colour of the RCMP ; the law enforcers of this ever pleasant country.

ORANGE
- The colour of fire and furore that helped shape the nation into Canada. The fire of the Indian spiritual rituals that flourished all over the Canadian land before European souls arrived. The colour of the bonding of the multicultural people to unite and co-operate with each other to aid in Canada's development.

YELLOW
- The sun rays that stretch from sea to sea to wake up the nation every morning. The brightness of the sun to sparkle and encourage growth in people and in the work they do. Yellow is the colour of the grassland in the Prairies in which grain and other farming resources are discovered and used to fuel the economy. Yellow represents the brightness that awaits this nation in its growing endeavour.

GREEN
- Green is the vegetation and forests that fill up around the many bodies of water in Canada. It holds many resources in which Canada converts into economic growth. It is the base of the pyramid that supports our nation. The natural resources that harbour in the green growth of our forests and amongst the roots.

BLUE
- The development of Canada expanding from sea to sea. Blue represents the transportation ways of our people in which the rivers transport people and products which add to the growth of our rich nation. Blue represents the clear blue sky that hovers over Canada's future. For blue is the limit to which Canada can grow ; that meaning the sky is the limit to Canada's ever lasting growth.

PURPLE
- The colour of many flowers that represent friendship between the multicultural people in Canada. It represents sharing and co-operation in which different people from different places can interact and share ideas to help and strengthen Canada as a nation forever !!!!

MIXED
- When all the colours as mixed as one, you will get the colours that make Canada an independent nation from other countries. Each colour has their own aspect and their own meaning. May these colours forever flourish and contribute to the growing nation known to many as Canada.

By: Judy Ng

Judy Ng, 15, Calgary, AB

Oh Canada, our country,
Beautiful and free.
We work and play together,
In simple harmony.
Our mountains are majestic,
Our forests lush and green.
Our wheatfields and our wild life
   are like nothing you've ever seen.
Oh Canada, our country,
Forever you will be.

Christie Rutledge, 12, Legal, AB

Jill Rodger, 11, Rothesay, NB

Megan Mullaly, 13, Goose Bay, Labrador

68

EH

All Canadian use the word, EH
We've all used that word,
Along the way
It sometimes happens once a day
We just have to accept it, O.K.!!!
It's like when cows moo,
It's like when owls hoo,
We just have to accept it O.K.!!!
Why do we say this weird little word?
At the end of a sentence,
It's simply absurd.
Some guy started it
I don't know why.
It's almost a Canadian symbol,
Because of some guy.

Jennifer George, 11, Burlington, ON

David Beier, 7, Edmonton, AB

Tamryn Liebenberg, W. Vancouver, BC

69

Canadians are such friendly people. God has really blessed our country with so many kinds of flowers and colours. My heart feels happy when I'm in my garden or on my swing listening to birds. O Canada we love you so!

Meaghan McCrea, 10, Hampton, NB

I just came back from a wonderful trip to Quebec with my grandparents. The fruits and vegetables were so fresh and colourful. And the sound of all the people speaking French was so different but nice. I would hate it if Quebec decided to break away from Canada. It's such a beautiful province. That's why I like Canada because it has a lot of beautiful provinces. You could have a fun vacation without leaving Canada. I think I had more fun in Quebec than Florida.

Alison Ide, 12, Scarborough ON

Beautiful Canada

Rachel Walter, 6, Nassau, AB

Some people don't have families to love and to love them back because of the war and diseases. It's a shame and I wish I could do something about it.

Anica O'keefe, 12, Placentia, NF

I like being a Canadian, but I am a native. Actually, I like being both because BC has a lot of stuff. Cree people have Cree names and mine is Peasqaw, Deasq and Cupatoata. We have a ceremony where you burn some rocks and there is a tee-pee. It has a hole right in the middle. We put the rocks in the middle, and put tobacco on the rocks. And there is a thing called a pow wow. In the tee-pee we say prayers and it is very, very hot.

Natasha Araya, New Westminster BC

Amanda Vowell, 14, Oakville ON

70

Mario Clarke, 14, Ile de la Madeleine, QC

We try to keep crime and gun control down and not to have war. We also try to keep places colourful where war is unable to open your door.

When others are in war, we join, not to fight but to calm their hate.

I must confess that I'm very lucky to live in Canada.

Eric Miller, 11, Montreal, QC

Canada, I'm glad I'm here, homesick when not, but glad for a break...

Paul Webster, 12, Mississauga, ON

Canada has trees
Canada has bees
Canada has animals
Canada has mammals
Canada has flowers
Canada has towers
And most of all,
Canada has me.

Elaine Ford, 10, Hamilton, ON

"Proud To Be A Canadian"

In eighteen sixty seven,
Canada we became.
One by one the provinces,
Were added just the same.

On Nov. 11th we remember those,
Who bravely died in each war.
They fought for our freedom,
Which was no easy chore.

Later in history,
A new flag replaced the Union
Jack.
It was the maple leaf that billowed,
Without any slack.

Our nation grew,
We can be proud of our talents.
Our education system,
Is proving to be in balance.

Mother nature,
Has blessed our native land.
With favorable weather,
And a climate to withstand.

We enjoy all four seasons,
Each bringing something new.
In winter it's hockey,
Or riding the ski-doo.

We can't forget spring,
The prettiest time of year.
When the grass is green,
And the buds bring lots of cheer.

In summer we golf,
Or swim in a lake.
In autumn we harvest,
Or we're out with the rake.

In Canada,
An election's a major part.
Governing our land,
Is where we always start.

Electing a premier,
Is hard enough.
But a prime minister,

Is extremely tough.
We must figure out,
Who can do the job best.
We go to the polls,
And are put to the test.

Wild life is also,
A part of our land.
From seagulls to turtles,
Upon the sand.

And if you're lucky,
And look up high.
You'll see the "V" formation,
Of geese in the sky.

Refugees come,
From far and near.
Broadening our multiculturism,
And bringing their customs here.

We have all different races,
That come from far and wide.
Together we live and work,
In harmony and pride.

We can travel in Canada,
From the east coast to the west.
Enjoying the provinces,
And how each is unique from the rest.

Over the years,
Our country saw a lot of change.
From the telephone, computer,
To automobile
There's been quite a range.

And although the nation,
Seems big with complex parts.
You can't forget the love and care,
In all Canadian hearts.

We're lucky here,
To have enough to eat.
As in other countries,
A meal is a few grains of wheat.

And for all these reasons,
I am definitely proud to live.
In our fair country,
With all it has to give.

Shirley Myhre, 12, Pleasantdale Central, SK

Province House is canada's birthplace. I am so proud to live where canada was born.

Corey Byrne, 10, Belfast School, PEI

Alshan A. Dar, BC

Olivia Lees, 7, Richmond, BC

Dear canada I love you Beacose

Cos it is a good plase. And there are No wars. And that if your Grampa and Grama livin Canada you can see them.

Jordon Bailey, Gr. 2, Pt. Coquitlam

I'm Proud to Be a Canadian

Canada has landscapes and mountains
And oceans for fish
We don't have to go to Disneyland
to fulfill a birthday wish

We have everything that other countries have
Sometimes even more
We can go visit other countries
But hey, what for?

Some countries may think
That Canada is dumb
But we have something they don't have
We have freedom

Paul Zammit, 11, Sydney, NS

Chantelle Walker, 11, NS

Shannon Huitsing, 9, Edmonton, AB

Pawlus Matthew, 9, N. Battleford, SK

74

I looked out the plane window and sighed. I couldn't believe I was finally on my way. After three months of counting down the days, here I was. I felt a shiver of excitement go up my spine as I recalled all the wonderful stories I'd heard about Canada.

My eyelids became heavy, so I folded up my table top. As I dozed off, I thought about how lucky I was to be coming to this new, wonderful country. When the plane landed, the first thing I saw was the outline of the Rockies through the airport window. "Wow", I thought, "they sure are beautiful!". I stepped outside and felt the hot sun on my neck.

I glanced around and saw people of different races, cultures and religions. They had on Calgary Stampede t-shirts, Toronto Raptors hats, Blue Jays t-shirts and Montreal Canadiens shorts. Everywhere I went people waved and were friendly. The parks were clean and I had a feeling of safety as I walked the streets.

When I awoke we were landing in Canada! "What a great dream.", I thought. The second we landed I stepped outside and gasped. Everything was just like my dream. As I walked through the crowded street, I thought, "This is paradise. To me, this is Shangrila."

Kate McPherson, 12, Dartmouth, NS

Why Canada is a Good Place to Live

Stephanie used to live in Bosnia,
And while she was there, she couldn't feel safe,
Then she came to Canada...
And now she can go to bed and not worry about never waking up.

Bobby used to live in Russia,
And while he lived there he could barely ever eat.
Then he came to Canada...
And now he won't starve

Sara used to live in China
And while she was there she couldn't have more than two children
Then she came to Canada...
And now she can have as many kids as she wants.

Ronnie used to live in Syria,
And while she was there, she tried to get out
But she couldn't...
So she fought and fought
Then she came to Canada...
And now she can go wherever she wants...
But she doesn't want to.

Lisa King, 9, Brampton, ON

Rina Sherwood, 11, Youngs Cove Road, NB

75

Karine Bilodeau, 15, Farnham, QC

Katharina Spotzl, 8, N. Vancouver, BC

Le CANADA EST BON
IL EST TRÈS GRAND.

IL Y A PLUSIEURS
ATTRACTIONS TOURISTIQUES
ET NOTRE BON
SYSTÈME JURIDIQUE.

NOUS AVONS   2 LANGUES,   LES HABITANTS
VIENNENT   DE TOUS   LE MONDE.

HOCKEY EST UN BON SPORT, QUE NOUS JOUONS
DEHORS!

LA NIVEAU DE CRIME EST BAS,
C'EST TRÈS SAUF, OH-LÀ-LÀ!

LA CANADA EST BON,
LA CANADA EST GRAND.

Dayton Ball, 14, Oakville, ON

Theis book is what a like, people caring about other people opinions

Matt Brown, Gr. 3, BC

We have a good Prime Minister, Fireman to stop stuff from burning. We are lucky because people share stuff with us.

Adam Ferguson, 8, Sydney, NS

My dad has a new liver. Thank you, thank you, Canada. He saw me be six.

I Love Canada

Alisha Cooper, 6, Waterford, ON

Paul Havas, 7, Hampstead, QC

Canada

Quel est ce bruit? Tu ne sait pas ce bruit? C'est un cheval.

Quel est ce bruit? tu ne sait pas ce Bruit? C'est les buffles.

Quel est ce bruit? Tu ne sait pas ce bruit? C'est des enfants qui jouent, qui prennent

des fleurs et qui sourient.

Jennifer Caldwell, 8, Richmond, BC

I look beyond my backyard and know that it will not last.
My parents tell of days when they went swimming in the river down by the road and I know that time has past.
It is hard for me to imagine walking with a towel around my neck.
And I know if we were careful it might turn around and not be a wreck.
I only hope that these dreams are not impossible and can still come true.
For I am but a few years old and would like to swim in you.

Take care Canada. I love you so!

Dale Crosby, 9, NS

Kali McLachlan, 9, Fort Smith, NWT

Canada is our home of the Algonquin People. We all love Canada and that is our only home.

Leighann Côté, 9, K.L. School, BC

Ken Young, 10, Richmond, BC

Oh, I love you so much! You are so clean, you have good weather and you are so big! Your grass is green and your lakes are blue. You don't stink. In fact, you smell rather nice. You have lots of animals and you're good to the environment. You have lots of factories and you make lots of shipments to other countries, and you receive lots, too. You don't have lots of pollution, like some other countries do. I like you just the way you are!

Oh, je t'aime tellement! Tu es si propre. Ici, le temps est beau. Tu es très grand aussi. Ton gazon est vert et tes lacs sont bleus. Tu ne sens pas mauvais. En effet, tu sens très bien. Tu as beacoup d'animaux et tu es bon pour l'environnement. Tu as beaucoup d'usines, et il y a des exports et imports aussi. Tu n'a pas beaucoup de pollution, comme on trouve dans les autres pays. Je t'aime comme tu es.

Heather Moulton, 10, SK

Lacy Albert, 11, Gallivan, SK

Michael Greidanos, 10, Edmonton, AB

I am very thankful for all the things that we have that other countries don't - like all the doctors and I am very thankful for hospitals that helped my sister's foot when she broke it and for the really good education.

Anne Pickett, 8, Saint John, NB

In Canada I like to live,
Many reasons I can give,
Country music I like to sing,
I want to be a cowboy king.
A rodeo cowboy would be fun,
Riding and roping in the sun,
I'd wear cowboy boots and a cowboy hat,
I'd saddle my horse and give him a pat.
I'd win that rodeo and a shiny belt buckle,
I'd be so happy I'd give a chuckle,
For now the city is my home,
I'll live in the country one day soon,
Until then I'll stay in my room.

Andrew Wilson, 10, BC

Canada is so clean! It makes me want to clean my room!

Kandace Stone, 10, Calgary, AB

80

Above the wispy swirls of fog that engulfs the wetlands, the crackling and chattering of Canadian geese can be heard - signifying the unity of Canada as a proud, accomplished, loving, a helpful nation.

Yet far away from the wetlands there lies a quiet, barren field that is exploding with beautiful blood red flowers called poppies. This reminds us of the courageous men and women who fought for our freedom as individuals in a war that caused pain, suffering and blood shed.

Now we, as either the first, second, third or fourth generation of Canadians are proud to say that - WE LOVE OUR COUNTRY!

Lydia Khoo, 12, Mississauga, ON

Beth-Ann Gowing, 12

Jessie C. Mackenzie, 9, Yellowknife, NWT

Brian Meindersma, 10, Edmonton, AB

Ici il n'y a pas de guerre
et j'en suis fière.
On a quatre saisons
et une belle maison.
Il y a de belles montagnes
et des campagnes
L'on est chanceux d'avoir des docteurs
et des belles fleurs.
Le Canada est beau
avec tout ses ruisseaux.
Je ne voudrais jamais
déménagé dans un autre pays
car j'aime mieux vivre ici.

Christine Boudreau, 10, Shédiac, NB

Canada, Canada you're so fine
You actually Blow My Mind.
Canada your so big You Make
Me do the Jigg. Canada Canada
your so Sweet you Swipe
Me off My feet.

Derek Cooke, 9, Windsor, ON

How are you? I hope you are good My name is Allison. I live on the west side of you. You are the most beautiful province in the world. Your what made my life happy. Your what Keeps me alive not dead. You Keep us cheer full and well fed. Your the best thing that ever happened to me.

Allison Farley, 8, Clearbrook, BC

Lincoln Dougherty, Barrie, ON

Nadine Alexander, 13, Wabush, LAB

I Love canaba becduse Theres lots
of things to Do You can Play
whatever you Want like
water Your garden And
IF YOU have NOThing to
Do You can JUSt go look
at Your garden.

Angela Shaw, 5, Langley, BC

Here's a big hug from me,
Canada!

Tessa Van Angeren, 8, Calgary, AB

Claire Delisle, 13, Longueil, QC

This poem is dedicated to my beautiful country and my loving mom, Yasmin.

Canada... a country of peace,
Never shall its beauty cease.
From the prairies and the lakes to the mountains so high,
The Canadian flag blowing proudly above the sky.
In the heart of Toronto (where the Blue Jays play ball),
the SkyDome opens to one and all.
It doesn't matter if you're from the maritimes or the B.C. west,
You should be proud to be a part of the country that is the best.
When I hear the word "freedom", I think of all those Canadian soldiers who gave up their lives,
To give us this free country we see before our eyes.
A word from the kids, who are our future,
Take care of our beautiful country and every living creature.
To be Canadian is such a great pride,
Aiming for a goal after each and every stride.
Before it's too late, stop the pollution.
We gotta put our heads together and come up with a solution.
I hope my words in this poem have made a difference
And soon enough all of us will be making a lot of sense.
From the bottom of my heart to the very bottom of my soul
I would just like to say : I LOVE YOU CANADA,
I LOVE YOU SO!!

Aliya Ladha, 11, Toronto, ON

I love Canada because it is a big country. I love Canada because it has lots of rain and snow.

Huong Tran, Gr. 2, Edmonton, AB

From children of the Gravenhurst Public School, French Immersion

Scott Holmes, 10, Nicole Vivian, 11, & Adam Robbins, 11, Gravenhurst, ON

Cher Canada
Tes forces me font grandir,
Et aller au bout pour finir
Ton pouvoir,
Me donne l'espoir.

Ici il y a des fleurs
D'autre gents de d'autres pays pleurent
La guèrre il en n'en pas
Les gens s'en apercoivent pas.
C'est le temps de s'apercevoir que beau pays

Lilianne Levesque, 10, Mgr-F-B

Canada I like it because...
there's a beautiful sun,
there's no tornado, there's
water and there's me!

Natalie Trainor, 9, D.D.O., QC

Josh Rotobilsky, 11, Kitchener, ON

"Canada Rap"

Canada is a real cool place
So let's talk about its oceans and lakes.
People are polluting and people are looting
So let's all do our part to keep Canada a work of art.
There's some violence but also silence
and peace for all Canada
So let's keep it that way, heh!

Jillian Schmidt, 10, North Battleford, SK

I love all the beautiful resources you produce. But not that smelly sulfur!
I love all your sweet smelling green grass I smell every Sunday morning!
I love all the beautiful birds chirping in my birdhouse on a bright and sunny cheerful Monday morning!
I love all the beautiful ski hills I ski on, on a Tuesday Christmas holiday!
I love all the Physical Ed. periods we have on a hot and sweaty really-make-you-thirsty Wednesday afternoon!
I've always loved your super slurpers at the 7-Eleven, especially on a hot and tiring Thursday afternoon!
I love to watch the X-Files on a warm and very cozy super special Friday night!
Uhh, Saturday night... forget it!

Tommy Enzel, Leduc, AB

Dear Canada,

How are you? You're probably feeling a lot of things right now. I bet each new day brings countless new feelings from Vancouver Island, British Columbia to St. John's Newfoundland. Happy, sad, confused, excited-with nearly 28 million people living on your soil, the emotional possibilities are endless. I am but one small voice among your millions and yet today I hold the one feeling all people across your vast entirety share. Today I am thankful, yes, thankful because up until now I never really realized how much you mean to me.

This morning at school I glanced around at the faces of my friends, and discovered that we wouldn't have met if it hadn't been for you. My good friend Azmeet just came to my school from India last year.

Quinton's family comes from South Africa. Jen has lived here all her life, but she is constantly bragging about her great-great-GREAT grandfather who first came to live on your soil from England on a giant ship with billowing sails. This discovery started me thinking about all the other things I have because of you. The scariest thought was that if it hadn't been for you, my parents would never have met. My Mom and her family moved here from Japan when she was only four years old because her father heard that you were a "land of opportunities". Boy, am I glad that you turned out to be just that because my mother was able to meet my Canadian-born father. If you hadn't been that convincing, I never would have been born!! (You couldn't know how grateful I am for this!)

My sister said to also throw in the fact that I am thankful for pizza, sushi, chinese food, curry and chocolate.

But especially, I love that feeling I get when I come back from some far-off place and see you greeting me-the feeling of coming home. Every single day, in everything I do, you are there-the soft sand on the beach, the park where I play ball and the very neighborhood where I live-EVERYWHERE, THAT GREAT CANADIAN FEELING. So Canada, I am your twenty-eight millionth emotion. I am THANKFUL. I thank you, for my friends, my family and all the treasures that you share.

I think that you're pretty special!

Love always,

Terumi Johnson, 15, B.C.

Katherine Swankey, Vancouver, BC

April Halle, 11, St. Clet, QC

When I first came to Canada it was like a miracle.

Noura, Gr. 3/4, Mississauga, ON

IM Soriy yor getting
Palootid. I will clinup
Asse muchasse I can.
you Helpmelive
YOU are MY Best
FRIND. think you

Natasha Fonseca, 6, St. Catherines, ON

I Like Canada Because of the Apple Trees and the pine Trees and the Lakes and the butterflies.

Rachelle Pullmer, 5-1/2, Vancouver, BC

88

Bienvenue, mon ami
au meilleur pays du monde
où tu peux faire ce que tu veux
penser ce que tu veux
exprimer ce que tu veux

Viens voir et je te jure
la beauté du paysage
t'éblouissera.

Mon pays, le Canada
avec ses 4 saisons
et 5 grands lacs
et couleurs magnifiques

Regardez l'eau, fraîche et claire et
le gazon, vert et brillant et
les milliards d'arbres
qui pointillent le paysage

Sens l'air, doux et net
sans pollution
sans maleur

Viens au centre-ville
où le soleil brille sur les bâtiments
en créant une lumière
fantastique
comme un arc-en-ciel

Viens à mon pays,
le Canada
et mon ami,
tu vas l'aimer

Juste comme moi. PAR:
VANI JAIN

Vani Jain, 14, Oakville, ON

I love you Canada because we don't have to put up with fighting. We don't have to go to the river. We just have to go to the tap.

Amanda Renaud, 7, Cut Knife, SK

O Canda I love you so much because your my frenied.

Niki Shah, 6, Mississauga, ON

Next time you are feeling sad, depressed or down
just remind yourself how lucky you are to live where you are now...CANADA

Eric Girard, 9, Vernon, BC

The world is like a giant ocean, and Canada is like a treasure box which you only discover if you look very hard, deep down into the heart of the waters. This treasure box is full of riches, hope and freedom. Canada is the warm heart of our world.

Melanie Bojkewich, Gr. 8, AB

Tyler Kirkland, 11, Calgary, AB

I like to live in Canada because I can go fishing with my father and grandfather. I can go swimming and I can go to the park. And I can also go the bed without crying from hunger. I like the kids who go to kindergarten with me.

James R. L. McLaughlin, 6, Grand Bay, NB

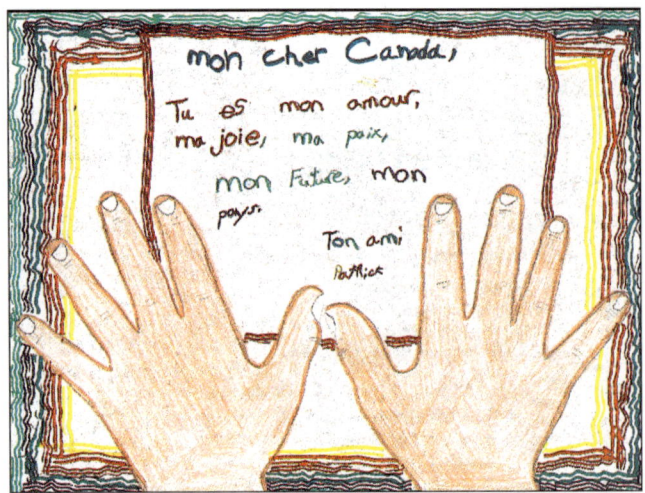

Patrick St-Jean, 8, Edmonton, AB

Canada is better then Hong Kong you have to do about three or four hours of homework each day in grade one. But in Canada you don't have to do a thing in grade one.

Ronald Li, Gr. 1, Vancouver, BC

Tyler Gelowitz, 9, Pierceland, SK

90

Matty Stewart, 5, London, ON

Je ne suis pas en danger parce
que tu me protèges.

Jodi Girard, 14, Falher, AB

Lauren Elliott, 7, LaSalle, ON

It's Just Plain Life

A fiery sunrise over wheat fields of gold,
A horizon of unobstructed view.
Turn around, see the Rockies, so stark and so bold,
A barrier hard to undo.

The wide river valleys, and undulating land,
Smoothing out to the immenseness of plains.
Each grain cultivated by a dependent hand,
Every field where the Ice Age has lain.

The dry summer wind is a memory when,
The harshness of winter grabs hold.
A landscape so cruel, the power dwarfs men,
And there's nothing in life, 'cept the cold.

The farmer's migration to cities and towns;
Their jobs have become obsolete.
For tractors and robots and mechanical arms,
Replace hands that were growing the wheat.

So thank God that one farmer looked under his soil,
And found the Plains' treasure-the richness of oil.

Mary Paterson, 15, Calgary, AB

Canada is full of green grass
And doesn't have too much trash
So don't destroy it
Or pollute it
So you can see it in the thousands
of years to come
Because Canada is for everyone!

Lindsay Atkinson, 11, Glace Bay, NS

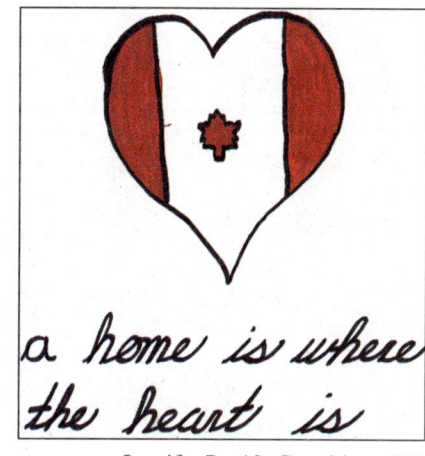

a home is where the heart is

Jennifer R., 10, Coquitlam, BC

91

Heather Goggin, 14, Fredericton, NB

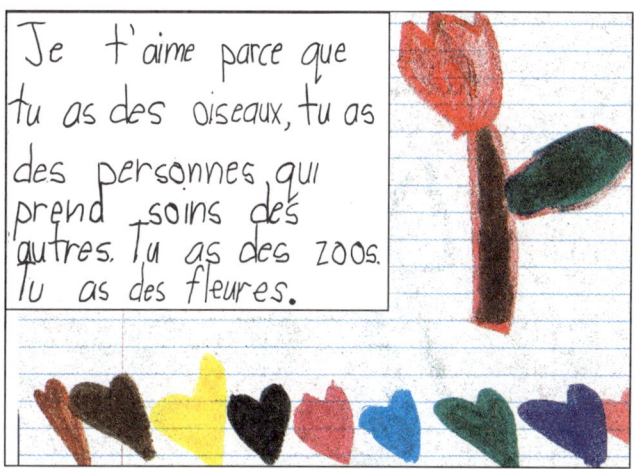

Eva-Maria Lima, 14, Montreal, QC

I think that Canada is the best because there are so many people living in Canada. Are you glad that we sing O Canada everyday? I'm that one who sings the loudest of sining O Canada. My friend Alysha sings the loudest with me to show that we love. Canada.

Tiia, 6, Mississauga, ON

To be a Canadian is to me an honour
I'm touching you every hour
You're one of the countries that's free
And you mean the world to me

Elda Merlini, 11, Bridgewater, NS

Je t'aime parce que tu as des oiseaux, tu as des personnes qui prend soins des autres. Tu as des zoos. Tu as des fleures.

Erin Huizinga, 6, Edmonton, AB

In Canada there is lots of peace and space. And there is lots of wildlife, too.

Garrett Mercereau, 9, Yellowknife, NT

I would like for you to fix these problems. To make the restaurants give all the leftover food to the poor people and take all the good beds from places that have been thrown out to the poor people and make more homeless people shelters.

It is sad that people have to go hungry.

Casey Fortin, 9, Vancouver, BC

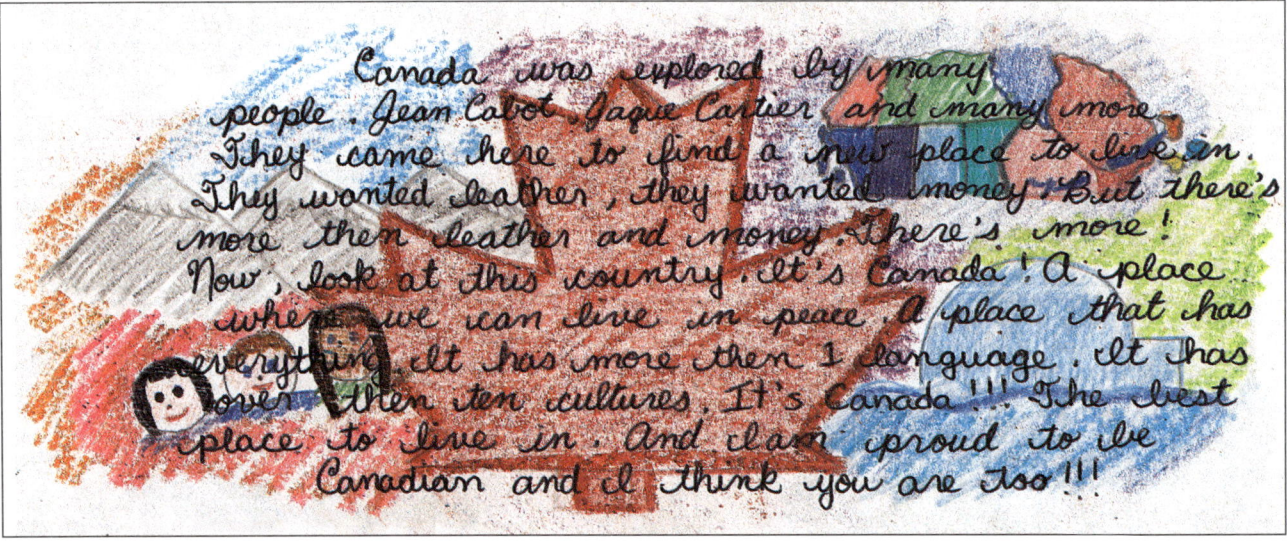

Canada was explored by many people. Jean Cabot, Jaque Cartier and many more. They came here to find a new place to live in. They wanted leather, they wanted money! But there's more then leather and money. There's more! Now, look at this country. It's Canada! A place where we can live in peace. A place that has everything. It has more then 1 language. It has over then ten cultures. It's Canada!!! The best place to live in. And I am proud to be Canadian and I think you are too!!!

Jessica Tjeng, 11, Hamilton, ON

Bryan White, 10, Kitchener, ON

94

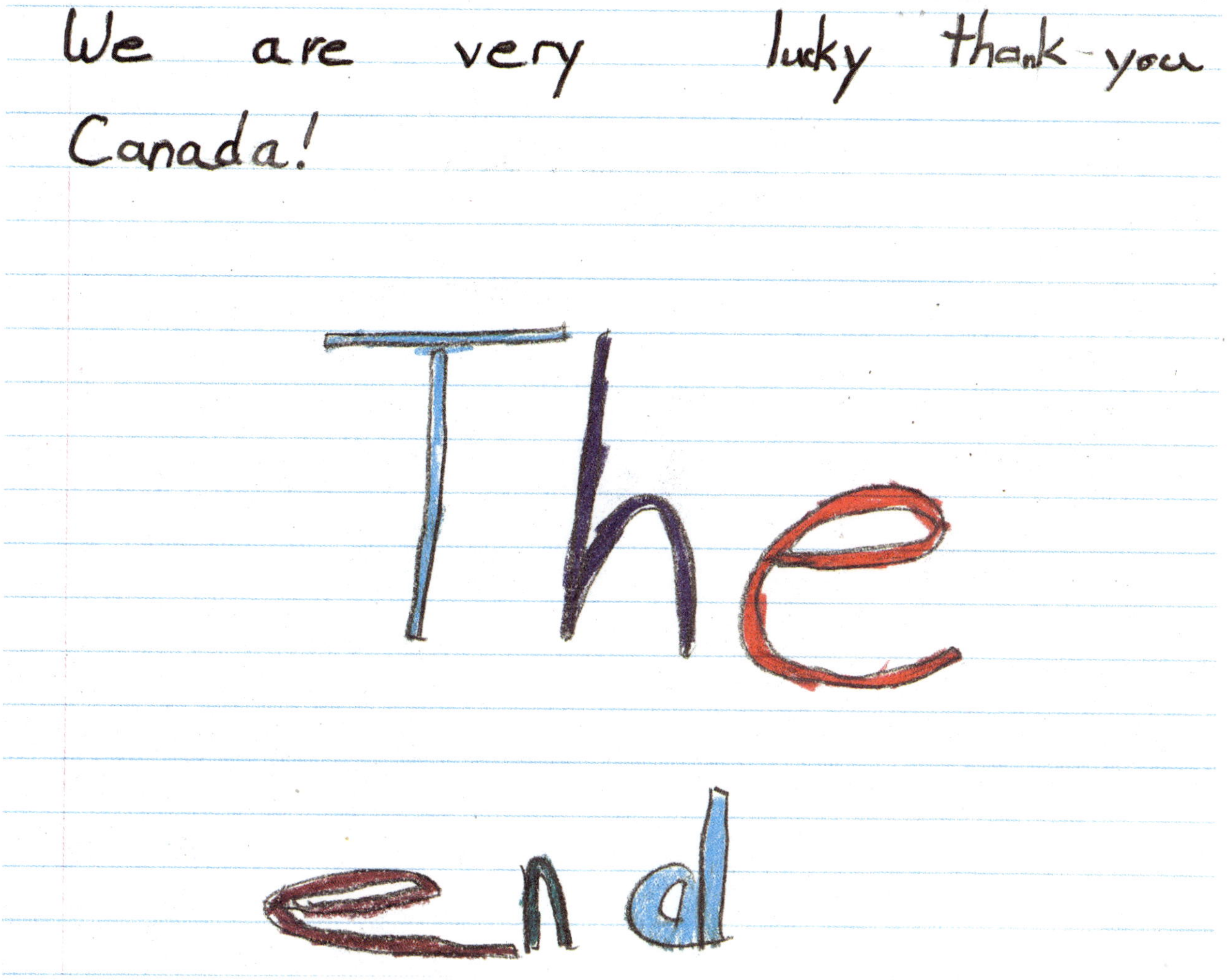
We are very lucky thank-you Canada!
The end

Amanda Renaud, 7, Cut Knife, SK

LA FIN

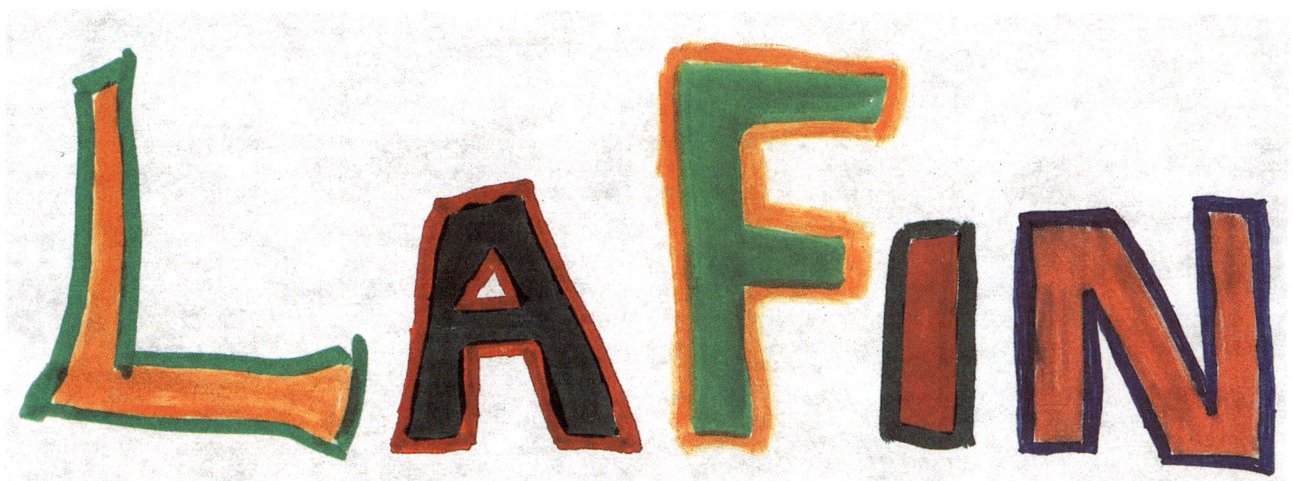

Catherine Dicaire, 6, Vaudreuil, QC

Our thanks to children everywhere who love their country and each other. The following few appear in the pages of this book :

Nous exprimons nos remerciements aux enfants partout qui aiment leur pays et qui s'aiment l'un l'autre. Voici donc dans ce livre les témoignages d'un petit nombre de ces enfants :

Adrian	Lucas Deschamps	Kelly Hunter	James R.L.	Christie Rutledge
Lacy Albert	Andrew Desjardins	Alison Ide	McLaughlin	Steve Ryan
Nadine Alexander	Catherine Dicaire	Jennifer Irvine	Laura McMahon	Elisha Ryhorchuk
Natasha Araya	Céline Dickner	Vani Jain	Erin McQueen	Jilian Schmidt
Lukas Archer	Angie Dinkel	Laura Jardine	Stephanie McGatey	Angela Shaw
Lindsay Atkinson	Lincoln Dougherty	Sara Jenkins	Kyle McGregor	Rina Sherwood
Christine Aucoin	Jeremy Dumont	Brianna Johnson	Trina McMullen	Darren Scheuer
Isabelle Aucoin	Kelly Durnford	Terumi Johnson	Kate McPherson	Niki Shah
Tristen Avila	Elizabeth and Linda	Justin	Brian Meindersma	Kavita Sharma
Anita Baidwan	Lauren Elliott	Kathryn Kane	Daniel Mendola	Tyler Speer
Jordon Bailey	Chris Ennis	Jennifer Kemple	Leif Menezes	Cassie Spencer
Lynda Bailey	Tommy Enzel	Lydia Khoo	Leon Menezes	Tommy Spike
Robbie Bailey	Alfred Étienne	Lisa King	Garrett Mercereau	Katharina Sptozl
Dayton Ball	Angela Eykelbosh	Tyler Kirkland	Wendy Merchant	Matty Stewart
Kimberly Barry	Allison Farley	Kitigan Zibi School	Elda Merlini	Patrick St-Jean
Aaron Beaudoin	Evie Farmer	Ava Kolodziej	Andrea Miller	Kandace Stone
Brittney Beckett	Sara Favel	Steven Koncan	Eric Miller	Kathleen Susak
David Beier	Marlyn Felaya	Jon Kornelsen	Jessica Laura Miller	David Sutherland
Karine Bilodeau	Adam Ferguson	Lloyd Kovacs	Jeffrey Mills	Katherine Swankey
Felicia Biondi	Stephanie Finlanson	Mathew Kuandibens	Audra Mitchell	Stephanie Szakacs
Roger Blackhall	Susan Fok	Lucas Kurztkowski	Fred Mooney	Marilyn Tardif
Mary C. A. Blagrave	Natasha Fonseca	Aliya Ladha	Anthony Morris	Alda Tavares
Christina Blair	Elaine Ford	Lisa Laflamme	Danielle Mossman	Melanie Thompson
Melanie Bolkewich	Emmanuel-Fortier	Pascal Laframboise	Heather Moulton	Renée Thunderchild
Janel Boone	Casey Fortin	Laura Lam	K.C. Mountjoy	Tara-Lynne
Christine Boudreau	Wayne Forward	Dan Lane	Megan Mullaly	Tiia
Elyse Boudreau	Tayla Fraser	Darcy Lane	Takako Murakami	Jessica Tjeng
Mary Claire Boudreau	Kristina Fredeen	Isabelle Larochelle	Alyse Murphy	Anna Tkachenko
Mélanie Boyd	Gerry Fung	Olivia Lees	Shirley Myhre	Jessica Torode
Colin Boyne	Juliane Gallant	Ali Leier	David Namkung	Natalie Trainor
Krissy Brady	Kathryn Galvin	Lisa Lemieux	Scott Neufeld	Huong Tran
Matt Brown	Annie Gaudet	Jonathan Lemmond	Judy Ng	Cindy Tremblay
Heather Buckley	Tyler Gelowitz	Lilianne Levesque	Tara Nichols	Trevor
Nadia Bujold	Jennifer George	Alex Li	Noura	Sara Turner
Kimberly Byrd	Eric Girard	Krystle Li	Anica O'keefe	Tessa Van Angeren
Corey Byrne	Jodi Girard	Margaret Li	Rebecca Oliver	Emma Kate Vetsch
Jennifer Caldwell	Ariana May Giroux	Michelle Li	Martha Overbeek	Jill Viejou
Desneiges Campbell	Heather Goggin	Ronald Li	Brandy Pakkala	Coreen Villamayor
Adlene C. Cappuccino	Zahra Goodarz	Tamryn Liebenberg	Jessica Pang	Kevin Villiers
Kristine Cassidy	Amy-Lynn Goodfellow	Eva-Maria Lima	Mary Paterson	Nicole Vivian
Jeffrey Cassie	Beth-Ann Gowing	Kay Linley	Gérard Patrick	Amanda Vowell
Daphne Cheung	Darrell Graham	Heather Lippold	Sam Pawliw	Chantelle Walker
Mario Clarke	Elyse Jean Graham	Jennifer Little	Valérie Perreault-	Tammy Lee Walsh
Milos Coko	Jonathan D. Grant	Mark Lovrekovic	Murphy	Rachel Walter
Michael Collins	Emily Gray	Lisa A. Lubenskyi	Anne Pickett	Paul Webster
Nick Commonda	Stephen Greene	Katie MacArthur	Catherine Pino	Allison Weekes
Emyle Connell	Shannon Greer	Jessie C. Mackenzie	Chris Polanski	Andrea Wheeler
Derek Cooke	Michael Greidanos	Tianna Macleod	Alexandra Pook	Bryan White
Alisha Cooper	Jeannine Guindon	Blaine MacInnes	Angela Possberg	Dana White
Cameron Cote	April Halle	Andrea MacNeil	Sara Powell	Jennifer Will
Casey Cote	Abra Hamilton	Corinne A. Mallonga	David Proctor	Andrew Wilson
Dustin Côté	Paul Havas	Josh Manitaoyen	Rachelle Pullmer	Jessica Winsor
Leighann Côté	Daniel Hawkins	Kerri-Ann Marchand	Jennifer R.	Marena Winstanley
Véronique Côté	Heather Anne Haxton	Jason Marroni	Amanda Rasmussen	Larissa Wodtke
Kellie Cottick	Laura Hendrie	Megan Martin	Svea Rawe	Derick Wong
Devin Cox	Mariève Héroux	Alicia Martinez	Alicia Reeves	Sarah Wong
Dale Crosby	Janet Hill	Rulie Marzyk	Amanda Renaud	Dicky Wu
Stephanie Currie	Troy Holloway	Roman Maslej	Adam Robbins	Diana Xu
Christopher Cusson	Scott Holmes	Pawlus Matthew	Jill Rodger	Yasmeen
Alshan A. Dar	Anne Hopkins	Amanda McConni	Josh Rotobilsky	Ken Young
Mariella De Ciccio	Lindsey Horsfield	Meaghan McCrea	Rebecca Routley	Matt Young
Gloria Decontie	Shannon Huitsing	Julie McIsaac	Amrita Roy	Patricia Yu
Claire Delisle	Erin Huizinga	Kali McLachlan	Brian Russell	Paul Zammit

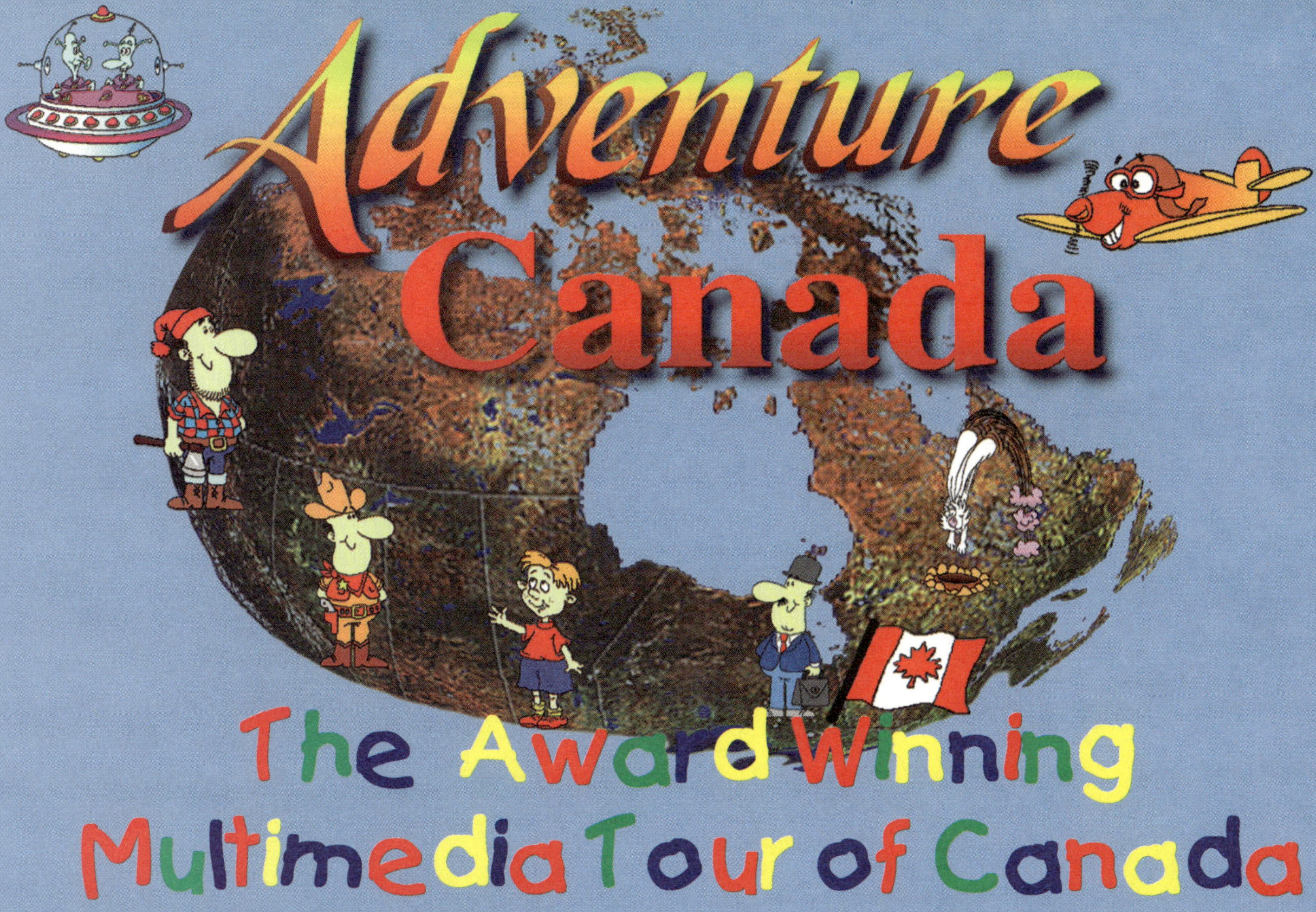

Adventure Canada

The Award Winning Multimedia Tour of Canada

Adventure Canada is a CD-ROM that allows you to explore Canada like never before. Point and click your way through the culture, people and history of Canada. With over **80 QuickTime ™ movies, 300 pictures, sound, graphics, maps, narration, music and animation** you will discover why Canada is such a special place.

Discover the ancient totems of Gwaii Haanas in British Columbia, Head-Smashed-In Buffalo Jump in Alberta, the spectacular beauty of Northern Saskatchewan, the polar bears near Churchill, Manitoba; the rugged topography of the Canadian Shield in Northern Ontario; the historic forts of Southern Ontario; the rich cultural mosaic that is Quebec; and the serene beauty at the home of Anne of Green Gables in Prince Edward Island. You will also better understand the powerful tidal bore at the Bay of Fundy in Nova Scotia, and uncover the secrets of the Viking settlement of L'Anse aux Meadows in Newfoundland.

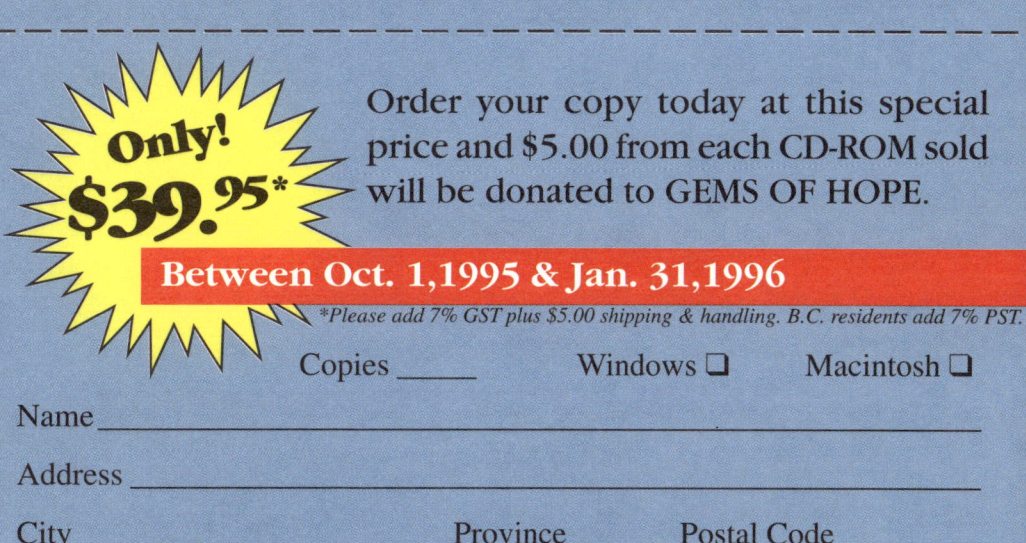

Adventure Canada

Winner of the Canadian Academy of Multimedia Arts & Sciences 1994 Digital Media Award for Education

Available Now !

Adventure Canada - French Version

What the critics are saying...

"... nicely done. Impressive engineering...a slick and enticing interface. A pioneering effort...undeniable charm ..." – *Toronto Star.*

"...one of the best field trips you can take...a wonderful combination of...geographic data, easy to use interface, and artistic photos and video, this program is one of the best ..." – *Children's Software Revue.*

"Adventure Canada is ... gorgeous and ambitious ... I salute the makers ... for the high calibre of their program." – *CD ROM News*

"★ ★ ★ ★   With its rich graphics, videos and map overlays, it is a must". – *New Media Canada*

"Every teacher and student who has had a chance to use your Adventure Canada CD thinks it is fantastic." – *David Styles, Computer Coordinator, Otter Nelson River School*

MAIL TO: *Virtual Reality Systems Inc.*

#1-12760 Bathgate Way
Richmond, B.C. V6V 1Z4

If this card is missing... Don't Despair!

Adventure Canada is available direct from:

Virtual Reality Systems Inc.

#1-12760 Bathgate Way
Richmond, B.C. V6V 1Z4
ph: (604)303-1200
fax: (604)273-6534
e-mail:
vrinfo@vrsystems.com